The
Akashic
Records

The Akashic Records

Blueprint for Your Soul

By Edgar Cayce

A.R.E. Press • Virginia Beach • Virginia

A.R.E. Press
215 67th Street
Virginia Beach, VA 23451-2061

ISBN-13: 978-0-87604-318-9

Cover design by Christine Fulcher

Contents

Foreword
Who Was Edgar Cayce?

Edgar Cayce (1877–1945) has been called "the Sleeping Prophet," "the father of Holistic medicine," "the miracle man of Virginia Beach," and "the most documented psychic of all time." For forty-three years of his adult life, he had the ability to put himself into some kind of self-induced sleep state by lying down on a couch, closing his eyes, and folding his hands over his stomach. This state of relaxation and meditation enabled him to place his mind in contact with all time and space and gave him the ability to respond to any question he was asked. His responses came to be called "readings" and contain insights so valuable that even to this day Edgar Cayce's work is known throughout the world. Hundreds of books have explored his amazing psychic gift, and the entire range of Cayce material is accessed by tens of thousands of people daily via the Internet.

Although the vast majority of the Cayce material deals with health and every manner of illness, countless topics were explored by Cayce's psychic talent: dreams, philosophy, intuition, business advice, the Bible, education, childrearing, ancient civilizations, personal spirituality, improving human relationships, and much more. In fact, during Cayce's lifetime he discussed an amazing 10,000 different subjects, and the

Edgar Cayce database of readings (available to A.R.E. members via the web) consists of a mind-boggling 24 million words!

The Cayce legacy presents a body of information so valuable that Edgar Cayce himself might have hesitated to predict its impact on contemporary society. Who could have known that eventually terms such as meditation, auras, spiritual growth, reincarnation, and holism would become household words to millions? Edgar Cayce's A.R.E. (the Association for Research and Enlightenment, Inc.) has grown from its humble beginnings to an association with Edgar Cayce Centers in countries around the world. Today, the Cayce organizations consist of hundreds of educational activities and outreach programs, children's camps, a publishing company, membership benefits and services, volunteer contacts and programs worldwide, massage and health services, prison and prayer outreach programs, conferences and workshops, Internet and online activities, and affiliated schools (Atlantic University: AtlanticUniv.edu and the Cayce/Reilly School of Massage: CayceReilly.edu).

Edgar Cayce was born and reared on a farm near Hopkinsville, Kentucky. He had a normal childhood in many respects. However, he could see the glowing energy patterns that surround individuals. At a very early age he told his parents that he could also see and talk with his grandfather—who was deceased. Later, he developed the ability to sleep on his schoolbooks and retain a photographic memory of their entire contents.

As the years passed, he met and fell in love with Gertrude Evans, who would become his wife. Shortly thereafter, he developed a paralysis of the vocal cords and could scarcely speak above a whisper. Everything was tried, but no physician was able to locate a cause. The laryngitis persisted for months. As a last resort hypnosis was tried. Cayce put himself to sleep and was asked by a specialist to describe the problem. While asleep he spoke normally, diagnosing the ailment and prescribing a simple treatment. After the recommendations were followed, Edgar Cayce could speak normally for the first time in almost a year! The date was March 31, 1901—that was the first reading.

When it was discovered what had happened, many others began to want help. It was soon learned that Edgar Cayce could put himself into this unconscious state and give readings for anyone—regardless of where they were. If the advice was followed, they got well. Newspapers throughout the country carried articles about his work, but it wasn't really until Gertrude was stricken with tuberculosis that the readings were brought home to him. Even with medical treatments she continued to grow worse and was not expected to live. Finally, the doctors said there was nothing more they could do. A reading was given and recommended such things as osteopathy, hydrotherapy, inhalants, dietary changes, and prescription medication. The advice was followed, and Gertrude returned to perfectly normal health!

For decades, the Cayce readings have stood the test of time, research, and extensive study. Further details of Cayce's life and work are explored in such classic books as *There Is a River* (1942) by Thomas Sugrue, *The Sleeping Prophet* (1967) by Jess Stearn, *Many Mansions* (1950) by Gina Cerminara, and *Edgar Cayce: An American Prophet* (2000) by Sidney Kirkpatrick.

Throughout his life, Edgar Cayce claimed no special abilities, nor did he ever consider himself to be some kind of twentieth-century prophet. The readings never offered a set of beliefs that had to be embraced but instead focused on the fact that each person should test in his or her own life the principles presented. Though Cayce himself was a Christian and read the Bible from cover to cover every year of his life, his work was one that stressed the importance of comparative study among belief systems all over the world. The underlying principles of the readings are the oneness of all life, a tolerance for all people, and a compassion and understanding for every major religion in the world.

Today, the Cayce organizations continue the legacy begun by Edgar Cayce with the goal of simply helping people change their lives for the better–physically, mentally, and spiritually–through the ideas in the Edgar Cayce material. Further information about Edgar Cayce's A.R.E., as well as activities, materials, and services, is available at EdgarCayce.org.

●

An Overview of Edgar Cayce on the Akashic Records

Imagine having a computer system that kept track of every event, thought, image, or desire that had ever transpired in the earth. Imagine, as well, that rather than simply a compilation of written data and words, this system contained countless videotape films and pictures, providing the viewer with an eyewitness account of all that had ever happened within any historical timeframe. Imagine, as well, that this enormous database kept track not only of the information from an objective perspective but also maintained the perspectives and emotions of every individual involved. Finally, imagine that this source contained not only information from the past and present but also constantly calculated probable futures based on current events. As incredible as all of this may sound, this description gives a fairly accurate representation of the Akashic Records.

Edgar Cayce, who has been called the most documented psychic of all time as well as a twentieth-century mystic, helped thousands of people through the use of his remarkable intuitive ability. For over forty years, Cayce gave readings, or psychic dissertations, using the Akashic Records as his primary source of information. Cayce's essential talent was his ability to access and describe information from these records–information that would enable people to discover everything from their essential purpose in life and their talents and abilities to the root cause of a relationship issue or any challenge that they needed to overcome. It was a source of information, Cayce claimed, which was available to everyone.

In an effort to describe how this was feasible, Edgar Cayce stated that it was not only possible for individuals to attune to the Akashic Records but that it was something that occurred frequently. Although the records were not physical in nature, an individual in attunement could "hear," "read," and "experience" the information, nonetheless. In order to illustrate what an individual might perceive while viewing this information, Cayce told an eighteen-year-old girl that the Akashic Records of the mental world was comparable to a movie theater of the physical world (case #275-19). This movie could be replayed in an effort to understand what had occurred in an individual's experience in any period, at any time, or while in any place in history. Also, within this data was a record of lessons learned, opportunities lost, faults acquired, and experiences gained.

In terms of the past, the Akashic Records of the past are associated with soul memory. In fact, Cayce suggested that "karma" was nothing more than memory. Just as a married couple may have very different memories about a past event that they shared, each of us deals only with our own karmic memory. There really is not karma between people; instead, there is only karma with one's own self. The conceptual challenge, however, is that individuals seem to come to terms most effectively with their own karmic memory, or "meet themselves," through their interactions with others. It is this interesting dynamic of meeting oneself through relationships with others that often causes individuals to perceive them as the basis of one's frustrations and challenges rather than accepting personal responsibility. And yet, in spite of the fact that karma belongs to oneself, each soul is constantly drawn toward certain individuals and groups that will enable that individual to meet self in probable circumstances and relationships. Those individuals and groups are, in turn, drawn toward specific people in an effort to come to terms with their own karmic memory.

In terms of how memory from past lives can affect us in the present, there are many interesting examples in the Cayce files, including one that deals with John Jay (1745-1829)–a figure from American history. As background information, John Jay was one of the leading political figures during the American Revolution. He sought stability in the new nation and favored continued close ties with Britain. He served the U.S. as a diplomat to both Spain and France. One of the authors of the Federalist papers, he favored a strong national government sympathetic to industry and commerce. George Washington appointed him the first chief justice of the U.S. Supreme Court. In time, he resigned from the Supreme Court and served as governor of New York.

During the Continental Congress, Jay was apparently in a tavern and noticed a beautiful young woman who was working as a waitress. He commented to Colonel Morris, his companion, that she was one of the most beautiful women he had ever seen. He stated that her beauty was partially due to the fact her face was the color of the inside of a conch shell. Apparently, the two men retold the story repeatedly at the Continental Congress–they had met the most beautiful woman in the world, but they were not going to tell anyone where she worked. The story became known as the "Conch shell beauty" and was so well known that it was retold in a biography about Jay: *John Jay: Defender of Liberty*, by Frank Monaghan (1935).

Prior to the publication of that book, a four-year-old boy was walking along a Florida beach with his nanny and stopped to pick up a shell. He asked her what it was, and she replied, "That's a conch shell." The little boy looked confused and an unusual idea entered his head and he asked her, "Can a person's face be the color of a conch shell?" Two years later that little boy had a reading and was told that he had been John Jay. That is karmic memory.

While giving a reading to a twenty-eight-year-old freight agent (case #416-2), Edgar Cayce tried to define these records further. Not only did he discuss what the Akashic Records were but he explained how they were written and clarified how an individual could gain access to the information. Apparently, any type of endeavor–whether action, thought, desire, or deed–creates some kind of activity of vibration. This vibration produces a mark upon (what Cayce called) the skein of space and time and is somehow permanently identified with the individual responsible. Although unseen, it is an etheric energy that is as evident to a sensitive as the printed word is to a sighted person.

Since these records are so complete, so accurate, and so individualized, a logical question might be, *Just what is the purpose of the Akashic*

Records in the first place? Simply put, the answer has to do with keeping track of and assisting with each soul's personal growth and transformation. Interestingly enough, the Bible refers to these Akashic Records as "the Book of Life" and suggests that the deeds of the soul are essentially judged by that which is written in the Book of Life.

The Edgar Cayce readings describe how each of us writes the stories of our lives through our thoughts, our deeds, and our interactions with other people. Our karmic memory of others does not destine the outcome of any relationship; instead it provides an "energetic impact" upon our subconscious thought-processes. In other words, we have to deal with our own subconscious feelings in our encounters with other people even when those feelings do not necessarily have their roots in the present. Everyone has encountered this dynamic, even though he or she may not be aware of it. It is easy to become conscious of these experiences because they essentially entail emotional responses to a situation (positive or negative) that are more emotionally charged or more heightened than the situation itself.

Essentially, Edgar Cayce's cosmology of the entire universe can be summed up as follows: *God is essentially love and the Universe is completely orderly.* Beyond that concept is the premise that each individual was purposefully created, as a soul, to become a companion with the Creator. Life did not begin at the moment of physical birth, rather there was an existence in spirit prior to physicality. God gave to each soul complete freedom of choice and the opportunity to find expression–to find self so to speak. Because souls were created in God's image, it would be only through a process of personal experiences–one choice leading to another, and then another, and then another–that God's companions could gain their own individuality, truly being a part of Him and yet individuals in their own right. Once they had discovered their individuality, they would once again return in consciousness to be His companions and co-creators.

According to the readings, the soul, basically creative in nature, longs to find self-expression. In fact, the essential question repeatedly posed by the soul might be: *Who Am I?* This question is addressed in infinite ways as each soul chooses specific experiences to meet itself. The soul gains firsthand knowledge not only about its own identity but also learns how choices may lead to certain experiences. In time, soul experiences and acquired knowledge will lead to wisdom. Inevitably, wisdom will lead to compassion and eventually love will be the end result. At this point, the soul will know its individual identity as well as its true relationship with God. The soul will have come to understand that its primary essence and God's are one and the same, *LOVE*.

For its own part, the soul finds itself in a physical body in an attempt to experience the dynamics of cause and effect, eventually learning to manifest perfect love, and, in time, becoming a fit companion for the Creator. The Akashic Records are essentially our personal tool for keeping track of the lessons we have learned and still need to master on the soul's wholeness curriculum. Ultimately, where is all of this leading? Why are we supposed to be working on loving one another and dealing with issues we have with one another? The answer is so that we can become worthy companions of an all-loving Creator. The soul is destined to grow (and eventually awaken) to an awareness of its true relationship to God. Whatever it takes to bring about this growth in consciousness is exactly what the Akashic Records will continually draw toward the soul. Cayce asked one individual, how much longer "can the will of man continue to defy its Maker?" (826-8)

Kevin J. Todeschi, author
Edgar Cayce on the Akashic Records,
and Executive Director & CEO
Edgar Cayce's A.R.E. / Atlantic University

1

●

The Nature of the Akashic Records

12/14/33 Edgar Cayce lectured in Norfolk, Virginia on CONTINUITY OF LIFE, relating the following dream which he had experienced many times, since the early 1920's, when giving a Life Reading:

294-19 Report File

"I see myself as a tiny dot out of my physical body, which lies inert before me. I find myself oppressed by darkness and there is a feeling of terrific loneliness. Suddenly, I am conscious of a white beam of light. As this tiny dot, I move upward following the light, knowing that I must follow it or be lost.

"As I move along this path of light I gradually become conscious of various levels upon which there is movement. Upon the first levels there are vague, horrible shapes, grotesque forms such as one sees in nightmares. Passing on, there begin to appear on either side misshapen forms of human beings with some part of the body magnified. Again there is change and I become conscious of gray-hooded forms moving downward. Gradually, these become lighter in color. Then the direction changes and these forms move upward and the color of the robes grows rapidly lighter. Next, there begin to appear on either side vague outlines of houses, walls, trees, etc., but everything is motionless. As I pass on, there is more light and movement in what appear to be normal cities and towns. With the growth of movement I become conscious of sounds, at first indistinct rumblings, then music, laughter, and singing of birds. There is more and more light, the colors become very beautiful, and there is the sound of wonderful music. The houses are left behind, ahead there is only a blending of sound and color. Quite suddenly I come upon a hall of records. It is a hall without walls, without ceiling, but I am conscious of seeing an old man who hands me a large book, a record of the individual for whom I seek information."

Reading 1650-1

Upon time and space is written the thoughts, the deeds, the activities of an entity—as in relationships to its environs, its hereditary influence; as directed—or judgment drawn by or according to what the entity's ideal is.

Hence, as it has been oft called, the record is God's book of remembrance; and each entity, each soul—as the activities of a single day of an entity in the material world—either makes same good or bad or indifferent, depending upon the entity's application of self towards that which is the ideal manner for the use of time, opportunity and the EXPRESSION of that for which each soul enters a material manifestation.

The interpretation then as drawn here is with the desire and hope that, in opening this for the entity, the experience may be one of helpfulness and hopefulness.

Thus, in seeing self as it really is before the SELF, before the Throne, before the Universal Consciousness, it is the hope that this will bring a better understanding as to what the purposes of an experience are in the material plane; with the daily activities and urges that arise from material circumstance, mental attitudes and the work to be accomplished of whatever nature this may be.

Hence we find from the records, the astrological aspects or sojourns of the entity or soul between its earthly manifestations indicate that which has been a part of the entity's experience.

For as the tree falls, so may it lie.

Reading 416-2

GC: You will have before you the body and enquiring mind of [416], present in this room; also the information which has been given him through this channel, upon which he seeks expansion, clarification, and further information, advice and guidance as to how he may make practical application of such in his present life. After giving such a reading, you will then answer the questions he submits, as I ask them:

EC: Yes, we have the body, the enquiring mind, [416], present in this room, and the information that has been given respecting this body and the soul activity in the varied environs that influence the body in its present experience.

Then, in aiding the body to make a practical application of that which has been or may be given in information of such a nature or through such a channel, it would be well that the body understand as to how and from what sources such information may come; that there may be seen as to how practical that which may be given may be made in the self's own experience in this particular period.

When there is the thought or the activity of the body in any particular environ, this very activity makes for the impressions upon the soul. For, the soul is that body which lives on into infinity, and is the companion of the particular body only in a particular or individual experience.

As to the records made by such an activity, these are written upon what is known as time or space; much in the form or manner as are the messages that are of a familiar nature to the body in its present activity. As the instruments of recording are used, so does the activity of ENERGY expended leave its imprint upon the etheric wave that records between time and space that DESIRED to be put, as to that impelling or producing. Just as the figures or characters make for communications between individuals, so does the soul upon the pages or records of time and space.

Then, this body through whom the information comes being in accord or attune, by the subjugation of consciousness into materiality, becomes the channel through which such records may be read.

The interpretation of the records, then, depends upon how good a reader the body is, or how well in accord with the varied experiences through which the entity seeking has passed—or the records that have been made by that soul. Hence, there may be much more of a detailed record read of an experience through which both souls passed, than of environs that were not a portion of that soul so interpreting the activities.

But each soul as this, [416], has made a definite record just as clear as that which may be written with ink and pen or with any other type, style or form of transmitting or recording that activity of an individual soul.

Then, in using that which has been given respecting this soul's activity in the earth, that there may be the greater influences in the experience in the present, it is just the same activity as the training of a mind into those fields of activity that may be used by the entity or soul or body in its relations and dealings with others.

Reading 275-19

As we find, the record as is BUILDED by an entity in the akashian record is to the mental world as the cinema is to the material or physical world, as pictured in its activity. So, in the direction to an entity and its entrance into the material plane in a given period, time, place—which indicate the relative position of the entity as related to the universe or to the universal sources—then one only turns, as it were, to those RECORDS in the akashian forms to read that period of that builded or that lost during THAT experience.

Reading 757-8

Yes, we have the entity and those relations with the universe and universal forces, that are latent and manifested in the personalities of the entity now known as—or called—[757], as recorded by the experiences in the soul's activity and journey through the environs that make for those impressions—or those that become manifested influences or forces in the experience of an entity in its present sojourn in the earth.

Questions naturally arise in this particular experience of this entity as to how or in what manner the records are made of an entity's sojourn or activity in a sphere or space, so that there are the abilities of one to read or interpret same. Are they as letters written? Are they as pictures of the experiences of an entity? Are they in forms as of omens or characters that represent certain influences or activities about the earth? Yea, all of these, my friend, and more; for they are as but the skein of life itself, the expression of a divine force from the God-Father itself, making manifestations in forms that become manifestations in a material experience. For truly to be absent from the body is to be present with those infinite influences and forces that may act upon and be acted upon, from the emanations of divine influences that may be either visions as picturized, written as thought in characterizations from the various influences through which such entities make for the communication—whether in ideas or in characters that represent those ideas in their expressions as one to another. As in all forms of communicative influences from one entity or soul to another—in a look, in an expression of some portion of the anatomical influences or form, or from word, or from the turn as from the cut or form of eye, shape or form of mouth, the rising of the brow, or in any communicative influences—these either bespeak of those things that are for the aggrandizement of self's own motives or impulses, or are the expressions of that purpose, that desire, whereunto such a soul or expression or entity has been called. These are forms or manners through which such are written, as in the Book of Life; and may be read and known of men. For that which is done in secret is proclaimed from the housetop.

Reading 254-68

(Q) What is the significance of the experience had during reading [373-2] Wednesday afternoon, July 12th, in which Edgar Cayce saw himself travelling through water in a bubble and arriving at the place where he always gets the information—the old man with the books?

(A) To bring from one realm to another those experiences through which an entity, a soul, may pass in obtaining those reflections that are necessary for transmission of the information sought, it becomes necessary (for the understanding of those in that realm seeking) to have that which is to the mental being put in the language of that being, as near as it is possible to do justice to the subject. In this particular instance, then, to reach that record suggested by the suggestion itself—as of coming into existence across waters, the very thought of those present that it becomes necessary that that which is to receive or transmit the information must seek (as indicated by the manner in which periods, ages, dates, years, days are turned back, in arriving at the experience of the entity in a changed environ); meant that, the psychic influences in their activity with or through the physical forces of the body, must in some manner pass through the necessary elements for arriving at or reaching the beginning or that point. With the amount of water that is more often thought than of ether, what more befitting than that in the bubble the seeking forces should guide themselves!

Then, so becomes much that arrives in the material plane; in the form of pictures or expressions, that there may be the conveying to the mind of the seeker something in his own type of experience, as to how the transmission of the activity takes place. Of what forces? The psychic or soul forces, that are akin to what? The Creative Forces, or that called God.

So, the body in a symbolized form as the bubble arrives at a place in which there is kept the records of all; as signified in speaking of the Book of Life, or to indicate or symbolize that each entity, each soul in its growth, may find its way back to the Creative Influences that are promised in and through Him that gives—and is—Life; and finds this as a separate, a definite, an integral part of the very soul.

Hence symbolized as being in books; and the man the keeper, as the keeper of the records. Much in the manner as would be said the lord of the storm, of the sea, of the lightning, of the light, of the day, of love, of hope, of faith, of charity, of long-suffering, of brotherly love, of kindness, of meekness, of humbleness, of self.

So, in the materializations for the concept of those that seek to know, to be enlightened: To the world, long has there been sought that as in books. To many the question naturally arises, then: Are there literally books? To a mind that thinks books, literally BOOKS! As it would be for the mind that in its passage from the material plane into rest would require Elysian fields with birds, with flowers; it must find the materialized form of that portion of the Maker in that realm wherein that entity, that soul, would enjoy such in THAT sphere of activity. As houses built in wood. Wood, in its essence, as given, is what? Books, in their essence, are what? What is the more real, the book with its printed pages, its gilt edges, or the essence of that told of in the book? Which is the more real, the love manifested in the Son, the Savior, for His brethren, or the essence of love that may be seen even in the vilest of passion? They are one. But that they bring into being in a materialized form is what elements of the one source have been combined to produce a materialization. Beautiful, isn't it?

How far, then, is ungodliness from godliness? Just under, that's all!

Seek then, ye, in understanding as to where, why, from what source, there may be gained the experiences of an entity, a soul, through its journeys in this the odic sphere, or through that known as this solar system. Each portion of that one whole, in that we call life, as it uses the attributes of the physical forces of a created form manifested in a material world, makes a record; as truly as is seen in the cylinder of the plate of the phonograph, or as is given to the radio transmitter upon the ethers of a material world. Going out where? Only those become conscious of same that have attuned themselves to that which is in accord, or seeking to know—then—His will; for each soul, every soul, should seek to attune its mind, its soul—yea, its body-vibrations—to that He, the Son of man, the Mother-God in Jesus the Christ, lived in the earth. Tune into that light, and it becomes BEAUTIFUL; in that you think, that you are, that you live . . .

(Q) *Please explain the experience the next morning, Aug. 30th, while giving [257] business reading [257-119], in which he was going through—and surrounded by—blackness?*

(A) A razor is a wonderful instrument for shaving beards. It will trim pencils, but not many beards after—if used very long.

A pearl is an adornment, a thing of beauty, created through the irritation of that which manifests itself in a lowly way to those that consider themselves of high estate; but by the very act of irritation to its own vibration is the higher vibration created, or brings about the pearl of great price. Yet it does not look well in the sow's ear.

In the use then to which, through which, the soul of the body would pass to seek that as may be sought by the varied creations of man's activity in a material life, to what depths must such a soul oft descend to bring back that that may even lend an air of help to a hungry soul? Through such irritation, though, oft does the soul grow, even as the pearl. So long as that manifested, then, by the life in a manifested form, keeps pure, little harm may come. But once lost can never be regained; even as that given into the heart of every mother to carry to her chosen one the bloom of life itself—only once!

So, in the understanding of that as happens when through the shadows or the slime, through the darkness or through the grime, may the soul seek to bring to light that which will ease the burden of a hungry soul, it finds its hardships—yes, here and there; yet may he lead that soul to the heavenly stair!

(Q) [Submitted by Rev. Thos. D. Wesley Presbyterian minister]: What, where or how is the direct and immediate point of contact between the Personal God and the soul, of which contact the soul is conscious and certain?

(A) As the sons and daughters of God are personal, are individual, with their many attributes that are characteristics, personalities or individualities, so (as this then is a shadow from that from which it sprang, its Maker) must the Maker be individual, with its attributes and its personalities. And yet fill all of life as becomes manifested in the spiritual realm, the realm of the soul or the temporal house, the abode of the soul for a day. As the soul seeks, then, for that which is the sustenance of the body—as what the food is to a developing, a growing body, so are the words of truth (which are life, which are love, which are God) sought that make for growth, even as the digesting of the material things in a body make for a growth. This growth may not be felt in the consciousness of materialization. It is experienced by the consciousness of the soul, by which it enables the soul to use the attributes of the soul's food, even as the growth of the body makes for the use of the muscular forces or attributes of the physical body.

Where is the contact?

As ye seek Him, so does like beget like. For, ye are co-laborers with Him, if ye have put on the whole of His love in thine own life.

Feed, then, upon the fruits of the spirit. Love, hope, joy, mercy, long-suffering, brotherly love, and the contact, the growth, will be seen; and within the consciousness of the soul will the awareness come of the personality of the God in thee!

We are through for the present.

Reading 378-13

Oft may it occur to one seeking such understandings, that may be gained through such channels, as to how such records of experiences are made; and as to how or why it becomes possible for only one here and there to interpret or read such records; and how that in the varied interpretations there may at times occur what appears to be a great discrepancy in the amount or character of such interpretations.

As the entity in its present activities is in that field which requires the consideration of pigment, or combinations of elements that act or react under varied conditions—especially those in which light, heat and other vibrations have much to do, (and as the experiences through the period being sought concerning were much, as would be termed in the present, the basis for that followed in the line of activity today) such questions are of particular interest.

Then, to draw a comparison that some concept may be gained as to the nature of records, and how they are recorded, and the manner in which interpretations are made, and the variations that occur, let's—then—for the moment put this in the language of that in which the entity is engaged:

(This aside. Don't think that you present will know very much more than you did before. He will!)

When a dye [die?] is cast there are basic influences that form that from which, to which, other things are added to take from or add to, to produce an effect that will not be acted upon by light, heat, moisture or the like, or other elements with the same. Yet, in the addition—to subtract from this first basis, there is always left that record in that which exists in the present of the dye, as to what basis the beginning was measured from. And in the interpretation, the analysis of what records were made as they were being put together, the interpreter oft loses sight of the base—of the addition—and sees the results rather than that activity producing same.

Just so in the soul life, the soul's contact with that which is conscious—that partakes of, or presents, or is represented in material form. The reading or interpretation of such an akashic record or cosmic impression, or such influences, depend upon the ability of the interpreter to meet in the same force, or attune into the same vibration, as to be able to translate or interpret the same.

Reading 262-105

GC: You will have before you Norfolk Study Group #1, members of which are present here, and work on the present lesson, copy of which I hold in my hand. You will continue the discourse on the lesson Wisdom.

EC: Yes, we have the group as gathered here; as a group, as individuals, and their work upon the lesson Wisdom . . .

Yet to thee, to whom the Book of Life—yea, the record of thine experiences—has been opened, there is the awareness that ye are indeed the children of God. And as children in thy Wisdom ye may approach boldly the Throne of Mercy. For the prayers of the righteous are heard, for they have attuned in Wisdom to the God-Consciousness within, and have come to the realization that they are not alone but that He walketh and He talketh with those who have called upon His Name, and who day by day show forth in their conversation their love. For Jesus is the Way, Jesus is the Christ, Jesus is the Mediator, Jesus is Wisdom to those who will harken to do His biddings.

And as He hath given, "If ye love me, keep my commandments; for they are not grievous to bear. For I will bear them with thee, I will wipe away thy tears; I will comfort the brokenhearted, I will bring all to those in the ways that are in the Wisdom of God for thy expressions through each experience, in each activity of thine."

For thy soul in its Wisdom seeketh expression with Him. Smother it not in the doubts and the fears of materiality but in the spirit of love and truth that encompasseth all, and that is open to ye who have set thy hearts, thy faces, toward the love that is in Jesus, thy Friend, thy Brother.

These, my brethren—yea, these my beloved children—Know that in Him is the truth, the light. Ye have seen a great light. Ye have touched upon the Wisdom of the Father, as is shown in the Son.

Then make thy paths straight. Let thy conversation, thy wishes, thy desires be rather as one with Him who thought it not robbery to be equal with God.

YE know the way. Do ye stumble in ignorance or in selfishness? Do ye doubt for the gratifying of thy body or for the fulfilling of the body-appetites?

YE know the way. Let, then, that love of the Infinite fire thee to action, to DOING! And indeed live as hath been shown.

Study to show thyself in body, in mind, approved unto that thou hast chosen in the words of Jesus thy Master, thy Brother—in dividing the words of life in such measures that all who know thee, yea that contact thee, take cognizance of the fact that thou walkest and thou talkest with Jesus day by day; keeping thyself in body, in mind, un-spotted from the world.

This is the Wisdom of God and is thine if ye will but claim it as thine own.

And may the grace and the mercy and the peace of a life lived in thine own consciousness be thine through Him that is able to present our lives before the throne of God spotless, white as snow, washed in the blood of the sacrifices made in our own daily experience—even as He has shown us the way.

Reading 281-33

Remember, all of these should be then in accord with that ye have attained to, that the Book of Life is given thee. What is the Book of Life? The record of God, of thee, thy soul within and the knowledge of same.

Reading 2533-8

(Q) *The Book of Life?*
(A) The record that the individual entity itself writes upon the skein of time and space, through patience—and is opened when self has attuned to the infinite, and may be read by those attuning to that consciousness . . .
(Q) *The Book of God's Remembrances?*
(A) This is the Book of Life.
(Q) *The Akashic Records?*
(A) Those made by the individual, as just indicated.

Reading 2144-1

The records are upon time and space, which are manifestations of that influence or force we call God. They are both old and ever new. But only in patience does the finite mind become aware of the VALUE of same upon the infinite, or the spiritual self.

Thus the records are taken from this skein of time and space. Hence, as an entity enters and leaves consciousness in materiality, there is left upon time and space that which has been the activity—thus there may be the interpreting of same.

Reading 3976-16

(Q) *Explain from what sources this information may be obtained.*
(A) Conditions, thoughts, activities of men in EVERY clime are things; as thoughts are things. They make their impressions upon the skein of time and space. Thus, as they make for their activity, they become as records that may be read by those in accord or ATTUNED to such

a condition. This may be illustrated in the wave length of the radio or of such an activity. They (the activities, etc.) go upon the waves of light, upon that of space. And those instruments that are ATTUNED to same may hear, may experience, that which is being transmitted. Hence do not in seeking CONFUSE thyself that there may not be variations as to the interpretations of economic influences or forces that are being enacted in the thought and activity of varied groups. Just as either [ether?] program may be sent from any given activity. The outer world is only an activity of the shadow world.

Reading 1549-1

In giving the interpretations of these records, these are upon the skein of time and space. And O that all would realize, come to the consciousness that what we are—in any given experience, or time—is the combined results of what we have done about the ideals that we have set!

If these are in keeping with creative or constructive influences, then these are developing periods. If they are of the selfish nature, or with the lack of idealism or ideals, then there is the retardment—or the lack of unfoldment.

Indeed the life and the experiences about every soul are such that if individuals will but take the lessons, the understandings of nature as it manifests in influences about self, they will see that such are the expression of the individual self's unfoldment.

As an illustration: A bulb is an expression of life, of beauty, in its filling its place in whatever environ it finds self. Man CAN change his environ, by the thinking. The bulb cannot. But man may view the purpose of all nature, he may view the bulb and see himself. If the environ is that which tends to enliven, enrich by creative forces added as constructive influences, then the beauty, the richness of the expression is a growth. But if it is dwarfed by an influence which hinders, it does the best with what it has.

So with man, the retrogression or progress is according to the application. The soul of each individual is a portion then of the Whole, WITH the birthright of Creative Forces to become a co-creator with the Father, a co-laborer with Him. As that birthright is then manifested, growth ensues. If it is made selfish, retardments must be the result.

Reading 1402-1

We have the records that have been made by this entity now called [1402].

In summing the records here, from that which has been made, these are as the Book of Remembrance; these are the book of life.

Life is that influence, that which is manifested in materiality as expressing growth, love, hate, disappointments, sorrows, hopes, courage, faith; and those things that take hold upon the soul, that which is the everlasting.

And this book is written upon the skein of that ye call time and space.

These exist—each of these—only in the finite mind as that which represents the separation of the various growths or experiences.

Reading 1562-1

In giving the interpretations of the records as we find them, some little explanation as to how they may be read or interpreted might be well for this entity; as innately and manifestedly the entity has an interest in occult things and conditions.

The records of an entity are written upon time and space, as the skein of things. They may be called as images. For thoughts are things, and as they run, so are the impressions made upon what we call time and space.

Hence often there is confusion in the experiences of those interpreting for individuals their activities through any given period, in differentiating between that which was the thought of an individual and that which was the actual activity.

But if there is the intent and purpose considered, or that the entity has desired through any given period of sojourn, whether in the consciousness of the realms about the earth (or astrological aspects) or in the physical consciousness of the earthly sojourn, in reference to that which is not merely idealistic toward this or that thought or trend of thought but that which is constructive, THEN the judgment of same may be drawn by the interpreter of such a record for an individual.

Hence how much greater the necessity, in the interpreting of such a record, that the one seeking same hold within self those desires for that which will be towards a helpful purpose IN the interpreting of same—even for self! That such may often shade what is given is true, but it is ever the law of Creative Forces, as has been given, that God has not willed that any soul should perish but has with every transgression, with every condition, presented a way, a means, a manner for man's correcting same.

So that as may be interpreted for this entity is with that singleness of purpose that it may be a constructive, creative influence in the experience of the entity.

Reading 1608–1

Remember, the records of each soul-entity are written—or impressed—upon time and space, as you call same.

Thus we find them as emanations from that expressed. Just as emanations from a metal, a gas, a light or what not—these pass off into what we call space; but they are continuous, because they are a part of the whole.

The attempt then to interpret or to read such records depends much upon the attitude, the desire of the individual or soul-entity seeking to know same.

Yet the very desire of such may be overshadowed by the individuality of an entity, as to cause deflections from that which might be an interpretation for constructive influences.

For it is only the will of an individual that deflects its activity in its relationships with Creative Forces.

Reading 1681–1

EC: Yes, we have the records here of the entity now called [1681].

In giving the interpretations of the influences about the entity—(there are quite many emblems—a great many figures)—that chosen to be given is with the desire that it may be helpful in the experience of the entity in the present. Hence much of that which has been a part of the experience through the sojourns in the earth will be given, forewarning and giving the purposes and intent for the entrance of each soul into an experience. We would give then also the virtues as well as the faults; with the desire that these influences be used constructively, or that they influence the entity in making that choice in which the greater soul and mental development may be the outcome from same.

As to the sources, then—as to the records, then:

Each soul, each entity makes upon time and space—through patience recording same—that as may be indeed the record of the intent and purposes, as well as the material manifestations of the entity through its sojourn in materiality.

Reading 1743-1

By records we mean those activities, mental and physical, in the planes of consciousness; that make their impression upon time and space much as light makes its impression upon the same elements or forces or conditions that are called time and space.

Reading 1796-1

The records of the entity are upon time and space, and are a part of the entity.

Thus we find this entity—as each entity—is in the present the result of that the entity has applied of Creative influences and forces in every phase of its experience. Thus it makes for that called by some karma, by others racial hereditary forces.

And thus environment and hereditary forces (as are accepted) are in their reality the activities of the MIND of the entity in its choices through the experiences in the material, in the mental, in the spiritual planes.

The entity finds self then a physical, a mental and a soul body all in one; with its virtues, its abilities, its weaknesses, its intents, its desires, all prompted by something innate; and manifested according to the application of self towards the mental and spiritual attributes of the entity as a whole.

There are then those accredited signs or omens or indications of characteristics in the innate and manifested activities of the entity. But these are irrespective of what the entity is to do, or will do, respecting same.

In the interpreting of the records here, then, we find the entity from the astrological aspects is influenced not because of the position of the sun, the moon or of the earth in its relationships to planets or zodiacal signs or other influences. Yet all of these are recognized as a part of the entity's environment. Thus, as Mercury, Jupiter, Venus, Saturn and Uranus are a part of the entity's experiences in those environs, they have as definite effect upon the tend or trend of influence as does that the entity may study or peruse or practice in its daily activity, or feed upon in its physical endeavors for sustenance in material environs.

Reading 1895-1

But each entity makes a record upon time and space, through the very activities of that stylus, the mind. And to be sure, irrespective of what an entity—as in this entity—holds as its ideal, its ideal is that judgement by and through which it makes its own choice.

Hence as these records or interpretations are given, it is the desire to give the entity a premise, and ideal, that it may answer to that search from within as to how to make this experience more worth while in this particular sojourn.

Then as we find, the experiences of the entity in the earth become an influence just as the environs in any one experience, just as it is true that what ye think ye become,—just as what ye consume for the physical produces such experience in thy physical and mental life as related to the ideals, whether known or still latent.

Also we find that the experiences of the entity in the interims of planetary sojourns between the earthly manifestations become the innate mental urges, that may or may not at times be a part of the day dreaming, or the though and meditation of the inmost self.

Reading 1946-1

Yes, we have the records of that entity now known as or called [1946].

In giving the interpretations of the records, these as we find are as impressions upon time and space; and it is the skein of these—in patience—that one becomes aware of one's relationships with the Creative Forces ye call God.

In interpreting the records, these portions of same are chosen with the desire that the experience may be a helpful one to this entity; that it may become aware not only of its relationships to the universe and universal forces but as to the why of its entrance into the material plane, and how it may apply itself in this experience in view of that which has been built by the sojourns in the material, as well as those interims that are recorded as astrological aspects producing or bringing urges latent or innate in the experience.

The material sojourns become expressed again through the emotions, or the awareness of same; while the astrological aspects are expressed more in the innate urges through the abilities of deeper meditation, or the turning within for the comprehension—that are as promises in life itself.

As He gave, "In patience become ye aware of your souls; and as ye abide in me, as I abide in the Father, you may know the purposes with thee since the foundations of the world."

Thus these interpretings for this entity are those records as we find that bring urges latent and manifested, but these do not surpass the birthright of each soul or entity—the WILL of the individual as to choice of that which is the knowledge, or of Knowledge itself.

For these are as the birthright of the soul itself.

Reading 2072-8

As to the place of records—this is a place, yet it is everywhere. It, the information, to be individualized, must come from some source into some form to be interpreted in the experience of the seeker. As; ye have here a source through which information as respecting varied experiences or associations may be given that affects the self in the present. The questioning, or the ability to question, indicates the ability to answer in self. And these must follow a universal law. That which ever supersedes or is even an extenuation of spiritual and natural law, not only doubt but reject. And know, as He hath given in those witnesses as concerning the way, that these are not past finding out but are conditional—to be sure. One must, and should, prove self worthy, by the application of the universal law (and natural law) in accord with the spiritual purpose in same to be qualified, to be in the position to understand and interpret further into that man (because of his own denseness and selfishness) has called the wisdom of the age, or the mysteries of the divine.

To be sure, that which has disturbed this body oft, from the records that have been interpreted—and the entity has accepted or looked at with a longing—when, what and where, then, is the source of information, such as ye seek here and now?

What records? Whose record is being interpreted, or being attempted to be interpreted, that ye may comprehend that being sought?

The records are upon time and space, but these—ye say—are concepts of man. There is no time, there is no space; they are concepts. Then—where?

In individual consciousness. The individual consciousness arises from that faculty or that something called mind. Thus those of old have said it in these words: "My spirit beareth witness with thy spirit, saith the Lord of hosts."

Then, the record is thine. How, then—ye ask—may this individual ye call Edgar Cayce interpret same? How do I know such is a correct interpretation? From whence is same read? With what is there the interpreting of happenings physical, of associations with material purposes and desires, under those environs when quite a different manner or language was used in interpreting the associations and activities? Whence cometh such a knowledge to one individual, as to interpret the records of another through varied spheres of activity or experience?

Only as a gift of Him who has given, "If ye keep my ways, I will love thee, will abide with thee, and bring to thy remembrance ALL things from the foundation of the world."

Then, while the source may be entirely capable of bringing a full or complete knowledge, the answers must ever be according to the law just given—within thine own self.

These truths—not thoughts—consider; as ye seek interpreting of experiences and associations—as well as when ye read those interpretings by others that are guided or directed by their interpretation of their spirit of direction.

Reading 2246-1

The records each entity makes are written or impressed upon time and space; and through patience one may attain to the awareness or consciousness of same in one's own experience.

Thus may the relationships of the entity and the universal consciousness, or God, become more and more a conscious reality. Not that it may be even describable in words. For, words are merely a means of communicating ideas to one individual from another, while universal consciousness with Creative Forces is rather the awareness that bespeaks of life itself. And life in every form is the manifestation of that force called God.

Yet, as was given in those admonitions by Him—who in the flesh was a manifestation, or became the manifestation of that God-conscious-ness in the material world—"In patience ye may become aware of, or awakened to, thy soul. In patience, and living in that consciousness, I may bring to your remembrance all things from the foundations of the world."

These are indications, then, that this entity in itself may—if it choos-es—come to that awareness of its relationships to that universal con-sciousness, that Christ-likeness which is manifested by the relationships or dealings one with another.

For as each soul—not the body but the soul—is the image of the Maker, so with the awareness of the soul-consciousness there may come the awakening to the realization of the soul's relationship with that universal consciousness, as is promised in Him.

Thus the records of each entity are a part of the universal conscious-ness, and "Inasmuch as ye did it unto the least of my little ones, ye did it unto me." These are the channels, these are the records then that ever stand as that angel before the throne, that there may be intercession. For, as the spirit of the Christ is one, and the individual entity in its manifestations of thought, purpose and desire makes its awareness one with that consciousness, so may that soul awareness come. For, ye find thyself body, mind, soul. These three bear witness in the earth. And the Christ-Consciousness, the Holy Spirit AND thy guardian angel bear witness in the spirit.

What, then, have been the manifestations of the entity through the earth experience that have brought about this present state of aware-ness in this ye call time and space!

In interpreting the records, then, there are urges latent and manifest-ed that are the witnesses in the records as we find here.

Reading 2420–1

In interpreting the records as we find them here of this entity, there are influences arising from the sojourns of the entity in the material planes, as well as from the sojourns of the consciousness during the interims between the earthly experiences.

Not all of these may be indicated in this one experience of interpret-ing the records, but these are chosen as those that indicate that needed in the present, or that as may be applied in the present consciousness of the entity as to indicate growth towards the filling of that purpose for which the entity entered this present experience.

What then, ye may ask, ARE the purposes for a soul manifesting in flesh in ANY individual entity?

In the beginning, all souls that were as portions of the thought of God were given the opportunity for expression, as to be companions for that Creative Force—or God.

Hence—as the application of self in relationship to the individual abilities has brought them as individuals into the various relations and into spheres of activity, in some there have been growths and in some there have been retardments.

But He, the Father, has not willed that any soul should perish, but has with each fault, each failure, prepared a way of escape; and that knowledge, that way, lies within the consciousness of each.

Reading 2787-1

Yes, we are given the records of that entity now known as or called [2787].

A beautiful record!

In giving the interpretations of the records as we find them here, much of these we find too beautiful to be classified or even called experiences. For, there has been a growth of this entity throughout the material sojourns. Not that there have not been wanderings at times, but a growth and an unfoldment.

These records are written upon time and space. Just as light goes out from a candle influencing the universe, the light that goes out from a life influences all with whom it comes in contact—and grows, dependent upon the spirit with which it is tempered.

Then in patience these records may be interpreted.

Reading 2156-2

(Q) *Anything else that may be given at this time?*

(A) Anything else?!! WORLDS! Worlds might be filled with that as might be given! But let each of you here so live the Christ-Consciousness, as manifested in the Master, that you may be counted worthy to be even as those who would gather the crumbs of wisdom that will be manifested through this entity!

Reading 1904–2

Yes, we have the records here of that entity now known as or called [1904].

In giving the interpretations of the records as we find them here, these interpretations are chosen with the desire to make this a helpful experience for the entity; analyzing the urges and impulses in such a manner that there may be a greater perspective gained by the entity as to why this or that has been the experience in this sojourn—from what latent force or power these urges have gravitated; and to give, if possible, a greater impulse for the application of self towards filling that purpose, or accomplishing that for which the entity entered this experience.

All is not beautiful from some angles, yet harmony and music, love, and the abilities for attracting of others, have been and are the latent forces in the powers of the entity.

Thus the good may be made a greater influence or force, magnified in the rest of the experience, and those things that would hinder made less and less effective in the relationships with others.

Remember, these interpretations are given with that intent to bring the materialization and realization to the entity of the continuity of life, and that what we do in mind and body records or leaves its imprint upon the soul,—just as that one masticates in bodily functions produces the physiognomy of the individual.

Reading 564–1

EC: We have the body here, [564].

Now, as we find, conditions physical may be said to be rather in that phase of their changes where counsel and advice had best be given regarding same as to recuperative measures for the body.

To be sure, it may be asked how there may be such conclusions arrived at through these channels—or why there may be the information from impressions rather than from the body itself.

This body and its general attitude, [564] we are speaking of, is a good example of this. From whatever realm an activity may be viewed or read, that activity IS the more prominent or outstanding fact. Would one imitating a frog be able to croak as well as a frog? Would that in the worm be able to act as much like that man knows as electricity as that which passes through the earth in the cloud or lightning? Both are forms of electricity, but their activity may be viewed better from the activity in which their activity is manifested.

So it is in regard to a body and the impressions; for thoughts ARE deeds and leave their imprint upon that element in which, through which, the activity is carried on—and may be read!

And this body in its thought, in its manifesting activity of waiting, putting out of the mind and activity other things that there might be information given for same, makes a channel through which there may be the greater service (if it will be acted upon), to the very principles that are or may be constructive influences in the experience of the body.

For, to some the touch of the hand, the smell of the rose, the look of the eye, all are giving forth an energy that is using in its very activity the forces that are spirit—or a manifestation of that men worship as God in the earth.

Reading 833-1

In giving that which may be helpful to the entity in the present and in the application of those experiences in the earth, it is well that the entity consider the sources of such information and how that given is applicable in the experience of self in the present.

As it is understood and seen, all force, all matter, is motivative by force known as spiritual. While the body is made up of elements that are atomic, super atomic, gas, influences that combine, all give off their radiation, both as to the mental reaction and what the body-mind does about that reaction, and it is recorded or becomes a portion of the whole radiation of that phase or manifestation in which the entity is conscious at such a period. And it is recorded upon that known or experienced by a conscious mind as time and space. And it may be read even as the records of a printed page. Hence that which has been the thought, the activity of the entity throughout its experience in matter, in the gaseous forces, in the atomic influences, is part and parcel of the entity's being. Thus we are, then, the sum, the substance, of that we do, we have, or may think and do. For each entity has that imprint of the Creative Energies or Force that makes of it an influence that is seen, known, felt, throughout the universe. For it, the entity, is a part of same, with the attributes of Creative Forces or Energies. And in the material it is endowed with that to apply same.

The source, then, is the reading of that the entity has accomplished in the earth, and the influences that are activating upon same by its sojourns in the environments of the earth's associations IN time and space.

Reading 2610-1

Urges latent and manifested arise from sources within the experience of the entity. All of former appearances or activities of the soul-entity in other spheres or dimensions have left their imprint. And each soul gives expression of same, dependent upon the ideal of the entity and the expression of the urge whether latent or manifested by the ego of the entity.

For, each soul is that it has done about creative influences through its sojourns in the varied consciousnesses or spheres of awareness.

Reading 364-6

. . . for, as records are made, the akashic records are as these: Activity of ANY nature, as of the voice, as of a light made, produced in the natural forces those of a motion—which pass on, or are upon, the record of that as time. As may be illustrated in the atomic vibration as set in motion for those in that called the audition, or the radio in its activity. IT passes even faster than time itself. Hence LIGHT forces pass much faster, but the records are upon the esoteric, or etheric, or akashic forces, as they go along upon the wheels of time, the wings of time, or in WHATEVER dimension we may signify as a matter of its momentum or movement. Hence as the forces that are attuned to those various incidents, periods, times, places, may be accorded to the record, the CONTACT as of the needle upon the record, as to how clear a rendition or audition is received, or how clear or how perfect an attunement of the instrument used as the reproducer of same is attuned to those KEEPERS—as may be termed—OF those records. What would be indicated by the keepers? That as just given, that they are the records upon the wings or the wheel of time itself. Time, as that as of space—as inter-between. That inter-between, that which is, that of which, that from one object to another when in matter is of the same nature, or what that is is what the other is, only changed in its vibration to pro-

duce that element, or that force, as is termed in man's terminology as
DIMENSIONS of space, or DIMENSIONS that give it, whatever may be
the solid, liquid, gas, or what ITS FORM or dimension!

Reading 254–67

(Q) *What was the cause of not being able to obtain [355]'s Life Reading on Sat-
urday morning, June 10th, when attempted? [See 355-1 on 6/13/33.]*
(A) The inability for the active forces of the body Edgar Cayce, from
the cycle of psychic influence, to contact that record necessary for the
interpreting of same.

It would be well that there be reviewed much that has been given
through these channels, as to how information is obtained through
these channels. Much has been given from time to time, though—in
reviewing same—there may be some enlargements upon that already
given that may be enlightening to those present, as to their own sus-
ceptibility to such influence; and may also enlighten some as to a better
understanding of the laws that govern same . . .

Then, considering this particular channel and what takes place when
information of a varied sort is obtained, or obtainable, or unobtainable
through this channel Edgar Cayce:

As has been set forth as to the developing of the soul–entity through
material–earthly manifestations (Please watch the wording), there has
been a development for the soul–entity that lends itself (through natural consequence of environment and hereditary influence, from the
spiritual plane) to activity in the realms of psychic or mental forces.

Then, consider also that which has been given, that through the
subconscious or superconscious forces of the entity the manifestations
may take place; or from the superconscious or subconscious forces of
entities that may have passed into that designated as the spiritual realm.
Through these, or through the universal consciousness or cosmic consciousness from the very abilities of the entity Edgar Cayce to wholly
subjugate the physical consciousness as to allow the use of physical
organs that may be attuned to all realms that pertain to psychic or
mental or spiritual influences in the realms about the entity.

Then, that which wavers or hinders or repels or blocks the activity
through this channel when in such a state may be from these causes;
namely:

The unwillingness of the body-consciousness to submit to the suggestion as pertaining to information desired at that particular time. Or the activity of the physical in such a manner as to require the influence or supervision of the superconsciousness in the body, or ill health, at such a period. Or the mental attitude of those about the body that are not in accord with the type, class or character of information sought at that particular time. Or there may be the many variations of the combination of these, influencing one to another, as to the type, class or real activity of the entity or soul that seeks the information.

For, as may be surmised from that given, one that would approach the sources of the information with the innate and manifested desire that that which is supplied in information should emanate from a loved one in the spiritual realm, and that desire has kept such an entity in the realm of communication, and there are those combative influences in the experience of that entity so seeking, and the development of the entity of the channel or medium through which the information may be attempted is capable of such contact, is there not—as presented in Holy Writ—the continual warring with the flesh and the spirit? The continual warring also with the spirit or entity or consciousness that would control through such a period of information passing from one realm to another.

For (for further explanation), this should be known to all: The material realms or earth activities are as a shadow or a manifestation of a spiritual law, that may in its essence—when viewed from the realm of psychic or spiritual or mental influence—appear to be quite different; yet one is the shadow of the other. But in describing, then, as a shadow upon a material plane, there would be periods—according to the time of day, the position of the body from the source of light casting such a shadow—when there would be an outline that anyone would know that from which the shadow was cast. Yet at other periods the shadow would be, of the same body (material body), such that the description would not reach the consciousness of those even more intimate with the body from which such a shadow would be cast.

So, with that which may emanate through such a channel, there be many influences that have to do with the corrector of the shadow cast; remembering, too, that material things—or the vocal cords of a body, material—are being used as the means of transmitting that which may be seen of the actual or true body that is being described, analyzed, philosophized, theorized, or acted upon by or through that being sought.

Hence, there are laws that pertain to the activity; as to why there become periods when there is the inability of activity, or when the activity becomes hindered by DIVERS reasons or causes, when they are so called in the material plane.

As in this particular instance that is asked for, with this entity now known as [355]: There were, in the field or room at that particular time, feelings in the make-up (which means of the whole body) of those present that made for a deflecting of that being sought; as well as of the shadow cast. Or, there was the inability to reach that position, that plane, that sphere, from which the record was being sought as made by the entity.

What are the records, and how are they made, is asked, that they may be turned back and so read by any soul-mind or medium or channel? (Which, in its analysis, means the soul-mind of either the entity through which the information comes or that entity speaking or manifesting, whether in hearing, in visioning, in writing, in speaking; but, as given, to become a manifestation it must approach through one of the channels through which consciousness comes to those that reside in the plane that is seeking the information. See? Hence, called senses.) In this particular instance, again there were those conditions in the entity's mental being seeking the information that were combative in opening self that the real record might be read as made.

How is the record made? How is the record read?

In the material plane we have instruments that are so attuned through the raising of the forces in various elements of one or another of the consciousnesses that manifest in the material plane. As in the phonograph or the radio, or the prism light; or any of the activating influences such as in the stethoscope with its various acoustic arrangements for the activity of elements related to movements of various influences within the realm of man's activity in respiration, circulation, activity of contractings in muscular forces, tendon activities, ganglia reaction, and the like.

These are but, then (from our first premise), a shadow of the real realm in which the activity of life is recorded . . .

Then, the psychic influences or forces in manifestation in their various spheres are as but a type of needle upon the record; a type of acoustics in the recorded or de-recording activity. Or the power and the influence by its development toward the realm of the first cause, as to the power of the tube or of the resoundant or of the length of its activity to care for its reproduction.

Hence, out of tune by many of the channels that have been indicated did prevent at that time [355] from receiving that later given.

Reading 877-21

(Q) For what purpose did I incarnate this time?

(A) As has been indicated, as each individual. Let's begin from that premise from which ALL of these may be reckoned:

God hath not willed that any soul should be separated from Him, but hath with every trial, every temptation, and every ERROR, prepared a way of escape. That the soul of man enters, then, or incarnates, is that there is needed in the lives of those whom the entity contacts that ability of that entity to present those influences of Creative Energies as there needs be for the production of helpful, hopeful experience; or the fruits of the spirit. Hence each entity then, in its entrance, is to fulfill that which has been given, "As ye do it unto the least of thy brethren, ye do it unto thy Maker." Know these, too, present then to every entity, every soul manifesting or incarnating, the basis from which that soul must become active. That the EXPERIENCES of the soul in each appearance or activity in the earth, then, makes for either the stepping-stones or the stumbling-stones, is as is shown in the book of remembrance. Then, that ye may be a light in HIS name; that ye may become one with Him by giving to others that hope, that faith, by those activities to them that may bring a brighter and brighter outlook, and more adaptable for the companionship with, the work with, that Creative Force. For we all—and ye are as others—are gods in the making; not THE God, but gods in the making! For He would have thee be one with Him. Then when ye reason from these activities in thy daily associations ye find it becomes as was given of old, not as a formula or ritual, or that ye should cry "Who shall go over the earth and bring a message, or who shall descend from heaven or arise from hell that I may know—for Lo, He is with thee!"

2

•

The Akashic Records, Destiny, and Free Will

Reading 262–86
(Q) Is the body aware of the destiny of the physical body at birth?

(A) God Himself knows not what man will destine to do with himself, else would He have repented that He had made man? [Gen.6:6] He has given man free-will. MAN destines the body!

Reading 254–51
As to the attitudes, these may be only given as advisedly as respecting how each is to react or to conduct their own thought. As has been given, this is the choice, as makes God God—that His creatures are, of their own will, to be made one with the ideal as is set before them, or to conform to ideals as they themselves build. Hence the variations in human experiences—but the heritage of man is self-will. That made one WITH God is creative. That made in opposition is destructive.

Reading 257–176
(Q) Will he be able to testify entirely for [257]?

(A) Will tomorrow come, or will it rain Sunday, or will it snow in June, or this or that? These depend upon circumstance; these depend upon will of man; these depend upon contingencies that are continually changing every moment. The DESIRE to do so, yes, is existent. As to whether there will be influences that may hinder or prevent depends upon too many things. This does not forsee other than that as has been indicated. Coming events cast shadows, to be sure, but the will of man ONLY defies God!

Reading 276–7

What has karma to do with this body, then? What is the fate, or the destiny, of such a soul? Has it already been determined as to what it may do, or be, for the very best? or has it been so set that the activities and the influences, the environs and the hereditary forces, are to alter?

These indeed are worthy questions, in the light of that which has been given.

If there be any virtue or truth in those things given in the spiritual or Christian or Jehovah-God faith, His laws are immutable. What laws are immutable, if truth and God Himself is a growing thing—yet an ever changeable, and yet "ever the same, yesterday and today and forever"?

These things, these words, to many minds become contradictory, but they are in their inception NOT contradictory; for Truth, Life, Light, Immortality, are only words that give expression to or convey a concept of one and the same thing.

Hence, Destiny is: "As ye sow, so shall ye reap." And like begets like! And the first law of nature, which is the material manifestation of spiritual law in a physical world, is self-propagation—which means that it seeks self-preservation and the activity of the same law that brought the thought of man (or the spirit of man) into existence—companionship!

What, then, is karma? And what is destiny? What has the soul done, in the spiritual, the material, the cosmic world or consciousness, respecting the knowledge or awareness of the laws being effective in his experience—whether in the earth, in the air, in heaven or in hell? These are ever one; for well has it been said, "Though I take the wings of the morning and fly unto the utmost parts of the heavens, Thou art there! Though I make my bed in hell, Thou art there! Though I go to the utmost parts of the earth, Thou art there! Truth, Life, God! Then, that which is cosmic—or destiny, or karma—depends upon what the soul has done about that it has become aware of.

Reading 281-49

Then, it is not that the entire life experience is laid out for an individual when there has been received that imprint as of the first breath, or the spirit entering the body as prepared for activity in the material world. For, again, choice is left to the individual, and the personality—as to whether it is the laudation of the ego or cooperation with its fellow men, or as a consecration to the service of the Creative Forces in its material environs.

Reading 347-2

As the entity should understand, there is an influence; yet, as to an entity's application of self—it is as to what the entity, the will, the soul, does about what it knows or feels, that makes for weal or woe.

Hence, when self is guided by an ideal that is set, as to its mental relationships, as to things, conditions and individuals, the results are the builded influences; hence have their application in the experience of every entity in its journey through the material or earth experience.

In this application also does there come oft to the entity (and to many another under such experiences, or such environs) much intent and purpose (or study) towards that relating to what may be termed karma, or the destiny set, and what an entity may do.

What may an entity do?

There is set before thee two ways, ever; and the choice is given to a soul as to whether it (the soul) chooses that in keeping with the ideals set in Creative Influences, or God, making the will one with, not blaming Him with that which comes to self, but self—as to what has been builded, and what self does about His love, law, and experience—in every relation.

Reading 378-45

Man, to be sure, is free-willed and may of himself separate himself from the love of the Father, even as from the love of those that would aid and help and succor and comfort in times of stress, times in which it is necessary that all cooperate one with another.

Then, let that love be in thee that was in Him when He gave, "If ye love me, keep my commandments, that I may come and abide with thee," not leaving thee to struggle against the hardships, the things that make one afraid, the things that make strife, turmoil and distress in the experience of all—that are the fruits of the desire for self to be magnified the more; but let Him have His way with thee.

Reading 391-6

(Q) What is the working out of destiny in the present?

(A) This is rather large subject, young man, to consider? DESTINY, as ordinarily understood, is that, that which is to happen to a soul or an individual will gradually be brought about. In this many falter, as to what is the cause or what is destiny itself. Each soul, as a garment in the making, is made up of the warp and woof of materials that are gathered through the associations in the making. And when once made, whether into the garment that has its position as of an unseen yet necessary use to a soul, or body, or individual, or perhaps—perchance—through the making has WON a position of honor, in that it is to be that worn in the most momentous occasion of an individual's activity, as to what the garment does depends upon how WELL the BUILDER of same—as a soul—does with its destiny, or its soul; as to whether that position is to be one of honor or dishonor. Hence, what has been builded in the soul of an entity is that which gives it ITS opportunity for occupying that position of honor or dishonor. Yet the WILL of the soul makes use even of those things, positions, that have been of dishonor, as stepping-stones; or, perchance, through the will, may use positions of honor such that the soul becomes wanton in its very activity. Hence, every soul that recognizes within itself its birthright in its relationships to its Maker may make of its destiny that the MAKER would have the soul fill, through each activity—as an integer or as a single entity in its passage through material manifested planes or spheres. Hence, DESTINY is what a soul does with ITS will as in relationship to the Creative Forces. See?

Reading 416-7
[Note: reading given in October 1935]

As to the affairs of an international nature, these we find are in a condition of great anxiety on the part of many; not only as individuals but as to nations.

And the activities that have already begun have assumed such proportions that there is to be the attempt upon the part of groups to penalize, or to make for the associations of groups to carry on same.

This will make for the taking of sides, as it were, by various groups or countries or governments. This will be indicated by the Austrians, Germans, and later the Japanese joining in their influence; unseen, and gradually growing to those affairs where there must become, as it were, almost a direct opposition to that which has been the THEME of the Nazis (the Aryan). For these will gradually make for a growing of animosities.

And unless there is interference from what may be called by many the SUPERNATURAL forces and influences, that are activative in the affairs of nations and peoples, the whole WORLD—as it were—will be set on fire by the militaristic groups and those that are "for" power and expansion in such associations . . .

Tendencies in the hearts and souls of men are such that these may be brought about. For, as indicated through these channels oft, it is not the world, the earth, the environs about it nor the planetary influences, nor the associations or activities, that RULE man. RATHER does man—by HIS COMPLIANCE with divine law—bring ORDER out of chaos; or, by his DISREGARD of the associations and laws of divine influence, bring chaos and DESTRUCTIVE forces into his experience. For HE hath given, "Though the heavens and the earth pass away, my WORD shall NOT pass away!" This is oft considered as just a beautiful saying, or something to awe those who have been stirred by some experience. But applying them into the conditions that exist in the affairs of the world and the universe in the present, what HOLDS them—what are the foundations of the earth? The word of the Lord!

Reading 416-18

(Q) *When and where will I next incarnate and will I be associated with associates of this incarnation and whom?*

(A) Better get into shape so that you can incarnate. That depends a great deal upon what one does about the present opportunities. It isn't set for time immemorial as to be what you will be from one experience to the other. For, as has been given, there are unchangeable laws. The Creator intended man to be a companion with Him. Whether in heaven or in the earth or in whatever consciousness, a companion with the Creator. How many will it require for thee to be able to be a companion with the Creative Forces wherever you are? That is also a law. What ye sow, ye reap. What is, then, that which is making for the closer association of body, mind, and soul to Father, Son and Holy Spirit? Just as has been indicated in thy physical being—there are those tendencies for auditory disturbances. Ye have heard. Have ye heeded? In those, then, to be the applications, what becomes disturbing? He that heeds not, then, has rejected, and there is the need for remembering the unchangeable law: "Though He were the Son, yet learned He obedience through the things which He suffered." Shall thou be greater than thy Lord? Where will these occur? Where do you make them? The place where you art, is the place to begin. What were the admonitions? "Use that thou hast in hand. Today, will ye [if ye will] hear His voice, harden not thy heart."

Reading 510-1

In entering the present experience, and in giving that which may be helpful in the present experience, we would find that alone from the astrological aspects a great deal has been changed from those influences that are naturally—or have been accorded to—the activities upon the individual life through the position of the stars, planets, or even in the astrological aspects. For, will is that factor in the experience of each soul that determines whether it has responded to that it has set as its ideal such as to make for developments along those lines, or whether retardments have been the experience of such a soul-entity.

Reading 531-3

(Q) *Is it probable, according to a so-called spiritualist, that I will meet an elderly person who will help me in my life career towards financial success?*

(A) As indicated and given, such things should rather be builded from within. And if the soul merits such, through that it metes to its fellow man, it may bring such into the experience of the body. But to say it WILL happen—it can't be done! For, the Father Himself has given each soul that portion of Himself. What the soul does about his knowledge, about his abilities or opportunities, depends upon the will of the soul. Hence, as to whether this is to come to pass or may not come to pass—it may, my brother, to ANY soul. What wilt THOU do about the opportunities that have been and are being presented to thee?

Reading 556-1

For, as has oft been given, the soul is that which is to be made one with the Creator, through experience and through the application of that knowledge and understanding respecting the laws of the cosmic or God-Force in a material world. And what the soul, the individual, does respecting such laws, such activities, makes for that preparedness within the inner self for the companionship with those celestial influences that make for the directing and the associations of ideas and of conditions in the realm of whatever activity in which the entity finds itself.

In the present, then, the associations make for those conditions wherein and whereunto the soul must make its choice; as to whether things are to be viewed from the material angle or from the soul's development—that must live on and on. And the choice also makes for the realm of activity in which are those things and conditions upon which every soul's development must depend. For, will and choice is the gift of the soul—that it may make of itself that which may be in the closer relationships with the spirit of truth, of life, of light, of understanding.

Then, in counseling with self, we find that in whatever realm of activity the soul's relationships are found, the BODY—the soul—is subject to the environs, the laws, the relationships of that realm. Just as the experience of the body in its material relationships has found, under the various forms of ethics, the activities in political science and in the relationships of the various governmental influences, these change according to environ. So does the activity of the body, the soul, in its varied relationships find that it is amenable to environs. But what the soul, the mind, the mental faculties, the intellect, does respecting that it KNOWS and is able to apply in its experience respecting the soul's development or the laws of the creative forces or energies called God, in whatever realm, governs whether there is produced in self and in the soul that harmony, peace, understanding that makes for a contentment in whatever realm; not satisfied, no, but using—and with the abilities to use that in hand day by day, that here a little, there a little, line upon line, precept upon precept, there may be added unto self that which will bring the more and more awareness of that soul's development for the purposes for which it came into this special realm of activity at this time.

Reading 778–1

(Q) Will the entity stay in India the rest of the life or come back here?

(A) Apply that as has been given as respecting how the entity should act as regarding these. The entity is of its own free will, as was given. There are set lessons and truths as the entity may apply to self, and its duty to self, to give knowledge, truth and understanding, to others. Whether it takes far or near, apply self, would the entity build that necessary for the full complete development of the entity in this earth's experience.

(Q) How long will the entity continue in the present work?

(A) Until it chooses to change! As given, there are those forces being set about wherein these changes may come—these definite conditions as appear from those of forces from abroad and from near. Application of self as respecting these is of self's will, and not of that as is read in stars.

Reading 816–10

What then are the purposes for a material manifestation of the to-tality of an entity's experience through mind, spirit, into matter?

That the entity may become more and more in accord with that which would make the entity a part OF the First Cause, or Creative Forces that are manifested in the material world in so many ways or manners.

For Spirit is the natural, the normal condition of an entity. For hath it not been given, God is Spirit and seeketh such to worship Him, in spirit and in truth?

Then an entity's experience, or advent into material manifestation, is to make the paths straight. For TODAY, in the experience of EVERY soul manifested, is the OPPORTUNITY to make manifest that which IS ideal, in the experience of that individual entity.

That there is spirit, mind and matter is self-evident in the expressions in which one finds oneself by the very awareness or consciousness of existence, and of the varying experiences or expressions that may be had in its daily relationships, its daily experiences with its fellow man.

Other individuals are individual manifestations of THEIR individual portion of that Creative Force.

Then that there are ideal relationships in each must be self-evident, but—as each entity, each soul, is creative and self-willed, then WHO may draw a line but that consciousness that thy spirit beareth witness with thy Maker's Spirit, as to whether ye fulfillthat best demonstration or manifestation of thy expression in any given period or material manifestation?

For God is not mocked, and whatsoever a man soweth that shall he also reap.

Then, there are ideal relationships in the material associations, in the financial structure (which, sad to say, too oft is the judgment in material associations), and in the mental attitudes—yea, in the spiritual attributes.

And then, as must be seen, must be felt, must be experienced sooner or later the awareness, the consciousness that, only SPIRIT is everlasting, then the promptings, the balance must be spiritual in its essence in dealing with or judging the mental attitudes, the social relationships, the material experiences.

For unless they are such, how CAN they be EVER lasting or constructive in the experience of any individual entity?

For that which had a beginning has an end.

Then, as ye begin to show forth in thy relationships with thy fellow man the love the Father hath shown to the sons of men, by not being willing that any soul should be separated from Him, ye must—by the very manifestations—at SOME experience come to be a separation or a fusion or union with the Creative Forces; with the abilities—by will itself—to KNOW thyself to be thyself yet one with thy Maker.

Even as thy Pattern—even as thy Brother, thy Savior—who KNEW, as He gave, "I and my father are one—as ye abide in me and I in him, so SHALL ye know the truth."

And as has been given, the truth shall make you free.

Then in the counsel to the entity in the present, KNOW THYSELF and thy relationships to thy Maker and to thy fellow man, and He hath promised, "As ye abide in me, so may I abide in thee."

Seek, ye shall find; knock and it shall be opened unto thee. "Call and I will hear."

Is thy purpose, is thy desire then one with Him? These be thy tests. Do ye show forth thy Lord's death till He come again? In manifesting in thy relationships with thy fellow man the fruits of the spirit? Hast thou grown more tolerant? Hast thou grown more patient? Hast thou shown more brotherly love? Hast thou given of thyself, DENYING thyself that they who have lost hope, they who are wandering, they who are discouraged might be ENCOURAGED, find hope?

THEN ye know ye are growing in grace, in knowledge, in understanding of thy purposes in the earth.

Hast thou grown to be so they who meet thee day by day take thought that thou hast in thy mental self walked with thy Maker?

THESE ye answer from within thyself. These ye know, these ye understand. Follow in the way that leads to everlasting love, for HE is love.

Reading 830-2

In counseling with an individual entity there are many conditions that are to be taken into consideration.

While the desire of the mother to aid is natural, is right, there must be the realization that the individual has his own life to live—and that even the great desire to aid may at times become a stumblingblock to another individual.

Then the greater aid is to counsel as respecting his purpose, his ideal.

For each soul enters the material plane for the manifesting of its individual application of an ideal in respect to the Creative Forces or Energies.

Each soul is then endowed by its Maker with that of choice, with that birthright.

And to live another's life, and to direct or counsel even—other than that which is in accord with that of choice, is to become rather a hindrance than an aid.

Hence the prayers of self, the counsel of self as respecting those things that are ideal in relationships to Creative Forces.

For there are no shortcuts to knowledge, to wisdom, to understanding—these must be lived, must be experienced by each and every soul.

In counsel then, let thy yeas be yea and thy nays be nay.

The anxiety that has arisen in self has only unfit self, as well as oft brought confusion in the experience of the individual—the son; with the desire not to be averse to filling the requirements for the peace, the harmony—yet these bring oft to the entity confusions.

Rather then let that counsel be as given, in purpose, in sincerity. Insist that this be held as the ideal: SINCERITY in every activity, in every relationship. And whatever may be undertaken, do with all thy might, with an eye single to service to a LIVING God that may NOT in ANY manner be set aside.

For it is in Him that each soul lives, moves and has its being. And while a man may defy the laws of nature, defy even the laws of his Creator, he must pay and Pay and PAY!

For His purposes will not be defeated among His children.

And each soul must give an ACCOUNT of the deeds, of the purposes done in the body!

Hence in being sincere, in being in a purposefulness, in an unselfishness for both the mother, the son, shall be the attitude, the directing force. For these are well-pleasing in those influences that make for constructiveness in the experience of one soul with another.

And though our physical relationships may oft have the experiences or appearances of the desires for a MATERIAL advantage, for a material success—unless the soul and the real desire is founded in patience, longsuffering, gentleness, kindness—and most of all SINCERITY—we become stumblingblocks to others.

Reading 849-11

. . . For what is Destiny? The destiny of every soul is in HIM who gave the soul, that the entity, the individual, might know, might be one with that Creative Force we call God. And how, the manner in which the entity, the individual, uses the opportunities makes for whether there comes the consternation, the turmoils, the strifes that arise from self-exaltation, or just the opposite. For how hast thy God meted to thee judgements? Not other than in mercy as thou showest mercy, as thou art a portion of that. What WILL ye do with this man thy elder brother, thy Christ, who—that thy Destiny might be sure in Him—has shown thee the more excellent way. Not in mighty deeds of valor, not in the exaltation of thy knowledge or thy power; but in the gentleness of the things of the spirit: Love, kindness, longsuffering, patience; these thy brother hath shown thee that thou, applying them in thy associations with thy fellow man day by day, here a little, there a little, may become one with Him as He has DESTINED that thou shouldst be! Wilt thou separate thyself? For there be nothing in heaven, in earth, in hell, that may separate thee from the love of thy God, of thy brother, save thine own self! Then, be up and doing . . . for the exaltation of self and self's abilities and self's powers and self's own indulgences—these ye must lose in gentleness, in patience. For in patience, as He has given thee, ye become aware of thy soul; thy individuality lost in Him, thy personality shining as that which is motivated by the individuality of thy Lord and thy Master! Thus does the Destiny of the individual lie within self.

Reading 877-1

In entering the present experience, as we find, there are astrological influences that have their experiences in the urges in the entity's activities in the present. These are by some accredited as being because of certain positions at the time of birth, but they are rather because of the entity's or soul sojourn in those environs that make for an influence upon the manifestation of that portion of the entity's soul and spirit in matter.

As we find then, these are making for their experiences, or influence in the experiences, and they come not as that which is impelling but rather as the mental urge. And what the will does with the opportunity makes for the development or the retardment. And as from the beginning, choice is that which separates the entity from the Creative Forces or makes for its being one with same. True, as it has been written, nothing in heaven or earth may separate thee from the love of that Creative Force, thy God, save thyself.

Reading 900-16

. . . As has been given, man was made a little lower than the angels, yet with that power to become one with God, while the angel remains the angel. In the life, then, of Jesus we find the oneness made manifest through the ability to overcome all of the temptations of the flesh, and the desires of same, through making the WILL ONE WITH THE FATHER. For as we find, oft did He give to those about Him those injunctions, "Those who have seen me have seen the Father," and in man, He, the Son of Man, became one with the Father. Man, through the same channel, may reach that perfection, even higher than the angel, though he attend the God.

Reading 900-20

(Q) Are the desires of the earth's plane carried over into the spiritual plane?

(A) When those desires have fastened such hold upon the inner being as to become a portion of the subconsciousness, those desires pass on. Such as one may have in gluttonousness, or in any condition that benumbs the mental forces of the entity, for the subconscious, as given, is the storehouse of every act, thought, or deed . . .

(Q) Is it the destiny of every spiritual entity to eventually become one with God?

(A) Unless that entity wills its banishment. As is given with man, in the giving of the soul, the will, wherewith to manifest in the entity, whether spiritual, whether material. With that, the entity, either spiritual or physical, may banish itself . . . yet God has not WILLED that ANY soul should perish. Giving of will to His creation, Man, that man might be one with Him, giving man the privilege of exercising his (man's) will, or exercising His (God's) will to be one with Him . . .

(Q) Is there such a thing as fate?

(A) Depending upon what is meant by fate. All elements in relative conditions have their bearing upon every element in the earth plane, and the will of any condition being with mind may act against such condition.

(Q) When an entity has completed its development, such that it no longer needs to manifest on earth's plane, how far then is it along towards its complete development towards God?

(A) Not to be given. Reach that plane, and develop in Him, for in Him the will then becomes manifest.

Reading 903-23

(Q) Is my present development on the road to fulfilling my karma?

(A) MOST individuals in the present misinterpret karmic conditions. The development or destiny as karmic influences—each soul, each entity, should gain the proper concept of destiny. Destiny is within, or is as of faith, or is as the gift of the Creative Forces. Karmic influence is, then, rebellious influence against such. When opportunities are presented, it is the entity's own WILL force that must be exercised—that which has separated it or has made it equal to the creative influences in the higher spiritual forces to make for itself that advancement. Then in EVERY contact is there the opportunity for an entity, a soul, to fulfillor meet in itself or its soul self's association with the Creative Forces from the First Cause, to embrace that necessary for the entity to enter into the at-oneness with that Creative Force. Hence as for the entity's fulfilling, it is EVER on the road. As indicated, during the next three years, during the astrological and the coordinant influences through the earthly experience, the greater opportunity for fulfilling same is before the entity, [903] called in the present.

(Q) *In what material sense can I best demonstrate these truths?*

(A) Within self, within the abilities to eradicate this, that or the other influence that SEPARATES the inner self from being aware of the oneness of all force and power that manifests itself in the earth or in the influence about same. By eradicating that which doth beset; which means becoming more and more aware of the fruits of the spirit that are set by all: Love, hope, brotherly love, faith, fellowship. These are the fruits of the spirit. These the entity make aware of, that as the body thinks, as the body limits itself in any NEGATIVE influence, then it becomes aware in that direction. As the body embraces all as a positive influence or force, more and more does the growth come to the awareness of MAKING itself, the soul, at-one with the Creative Forces. See?

Reading 1235-1

(Q) *Please give in detail just what relation I have had with my present Aunt [268].*

(A) That which makes for the closer relationship was in the Roman experience, where the aunt then depended upon the word and activities of the entity in that experience. Hence it may be found in the present that those influences, those activities may become reversed in this experience—and the entity depend upon the word and the help of the aunt in the present. But unless these abilities are guided, unless these are kept, they may turn to turmoils—even as has been indicated HAS been the experience of the entity.

(Q) *What was the relation between the two in that period?*

(A) One depended upon the other. Friends.

(Q) *Please give in detail just what we should mean to each other in the present?*

(A) As has been indicated. These become reversed. One depends upon the other for direction. One depends upon the other now for the guidance and especially for the directing in the SPIRITUAL portion of its life.

(Q) Will our lives be closely associated or separated?

(A) This depends to be sure upon the activities—all of these. NO LIFE, no individual is set! It is not a line; it deviates. For the WILL of each may change the relationships.

(Q) Will I be much benefitted in this experience, and how?

(A) Depends upon the application again. EVERYTHING in the experience depends upon the application. How wilt thou use thy opportunities? if for weal or for woe? These are NOT set! They do not happen irrespective or regardless! Life is earnest, life is work, life is DOING; not having it poured out, not having it given—but work!

Reading 1437-1

In giving the interpretation of the records as we find here, know that these are urges that arise from the experiences of the entity through the astrological aspects or sojourns as well as from the appearances and activities of the entity in the earth.

Yet these, while making definite urges, and those inclinations for material manifestations, may be altered by what the entity does about same.

For there is the free will, that may change any activity. And that so often called "destined" should be understood; that there are the ways of activity—if they are constructive they become mental and soul building, bringing with same a joy, a peace not found in unconstructive experience, nor in the gratifying alone of selfish interests. For these oft turn and rend those that make of themselves or their appetites idols in their daily experience.

For he that would have life must give it. He that would have friends must be friendly.

If ye would have those that would believe in you, ye must keep promises, ye must realize the obligations; and these are oft too lightly considered in the experience of the entity.

Reading 1440-1

Yet if the lessons, if the tenets, if the life's activities are guided by those very things that were heard, and that have been pondered oft in the experience, and they are kept as the watchword, as the guiding light, as the standard of its ideal, there will come a greater harmony and peace into the experience with which it now deals.

For as is the purpose of the entity's experience in the present, as to others, that their lessons may be learned. For it is continually self being met, and what ye have done about it, and only the promises, the faith, the activity in those things for whom and from whom there has been obtained an advocate with the Father may mercies be shown. For only as ye show mercy may it be shown to thee. Only as ye show patience, longsuffering, brotherly kindness, may these be shown to thee. For thou art indeed a god in its making, for He would have thee as one with Him; yet the choices must be made by thee, or else ye become only as an automaton, only capable of doing that to which ye have been set as unchangeable. For while the law of the Lord is ever the same, the abilities to show forth same are according to the individual application. Good is good. There is not better good than GOOD.

Be not then merely good, but be good for something—in HIS name!

Reading 1531-1

For the experiences may be the lessons, as well as encouraging experiences that the promises that are within thine inner self may be assured of thy oneness with the Creative Forces that supply all of the influences that become constructive in the experience.

But ye being the co-creator with these forces, make with thy will and thy application of thy ideals the choices that bring about in the fruit of thy activities the good or bad deeds—or good and bad influences or manifestations.

These then are the judgements of individuals. For there is little within thyself that is bad, but according to its RELATIVE relationships to that which is thy ideal.

Ask of self, then, "What is my ideal?"

If it is founded in spirituality, if it is founded in those influences and forces that are constructive, then hold fast to same. Know in WHOM ye have believed, know WHO is the Author of thy belief of thy thought, and that He is able to keep that ye may commit unto Him against ANY experience that may arise in thy activities through any sphere of experience; whether within the mental self, the physical self, the spiritual self.

For thy body is the temple of thy soul, and as the soul is spirit so may the spirit of constructive forces meet thee there.

Then present thy body as a living sacrifice, holy, acceptable unto Him who is the author and the finisher of thy faith.

Reading 1538-1

In the application of the influences, know that these are but urges; the will, the desire and that which the self sets as its ideal—whether pertaining to the material, the mental or the spiritual forces—should be the guide, should be the measuring stick always for decisions that the entity may make in associations or in activities; whether these deal with spiritual forces or the mental or material activities.

And unless one does hold or set an ideal, one continues to be a drifter; and never is at peace with self.

For he that condemns himself, or others, is not wise. Rather is it that each should set for himself an ideal manner and keep in purpose, in desire, in activity to that; and the growth comes.

For it is the gift of Creative Forces in the experience of life in every phase of its manifestation, and is thus a part of the experience of the individual entity or soul in its sojourn through any given experience...

For ever, day by day, is there a choice to be made by each soul. One may lead to happiness, joy; the other to confusion, to disturbing forces, to evil and to self-condemnation.

But the WILL is of self, else ye would not indeed be the child of the Creative and Living Force or God that ye are; but as an automaton.

Then exercise thyself, and bring that to pass in thy experience that will create for THEE the environ of helpful hopefulness in the experience day by day.

Reading 1565-1

As to the abilities of the entity, and to that which it may attain in the present earth's plane—as has been given, in this year, 1926, will be presented those changes, which would be well to make, provided they would be only in that way and that manner as has been seen is best for the entity's development to make such change, and the entity's abilities lie in business of selling, of association with others in business, will the entity apply first those principles as are set in the way of the Lord, for in Him is the way, and in Him is the light, and the Lord is the Giver of good gifts to those who love Him.

As to those conditions that the entity be warned of in the latter portion of life, these, as are seen, are forewarnings. Then, being forewarned, be forearmed, for the WILL—as is the gift of the Creator to man, made a little lower than the angels, with the power of choosing for self as to whether the entity that is given in the body will be One with the Creator or attempt to set up self in that position of atvariance with that Creator, as is seen in him who made war in heaven—in this position, then, the entity must build for self. The conditions are set, even as the Lord has given, "This day I have set before thee good and evil. Choose thou whom thy peoples and thy self will serve," for the Lord is not far off, but is in thine own heart, and the manner and way that the application of self, and self's abilities, to those entities, those individuals, about one's self, is that entity's conception, to others, of that creative force. Use, then, that thou hast in thy hands, as the means to correct many conditions as have been builded within thine own self, and make thyself first right with Him and His laws, through the service that THY SELF may render to thy brothers.

Reading 1567–2

For as was given of old, there is each day set before us life and death, good and evil. We choose because of our natures. If our will were broken, if we were commanded to do this or that, or to become as an automaton, our individuality then would be lost and we would only be as in Him without conscience—CONSCIENCE—(consciousness) of being one with Him; with the abilities to choose for self!

For we CAN, as God, say Yea to this, Nay to that; we CAN order this or the other in our experience, by the very gifts that have been given or appointed unto our keeping. For we are indeed as laborers, co-laborers in the vineyard of the Lord—or of they that are fearful of His coming.

And we choose each day WHOM we will serve! And by the records in time and space, as we have moved through the realms of His kingdom, we have left our mark upon same.

Then they influence us, either directly or indirectly, in the manner as we have declared ourselves in favor of this or that influence in our material experience. And by the casting of our lot in this or that direction, we bring into our experience the influence in that manner.

Reading 1632-3

EC: Yes, we have the records here of that entity now known as [1632].
In giving the interpretations of the records here, these as we find are
in those positions of changes. Yet these are given with the desire and
purpose to make the experience a helpful, hopeful one in the application of that the entity has or may set as its ideal.

Remember, these records are the interpretation of that ye have
builded in thy mental, thy material, thy spiritual activities through the
sojourns of the soul-entity in the material world; through the relationships and activities ye have manifested towards others.

There comes then into the experience of each entity, through a material sojourn, the consciousness or awareness of its relationships to
others; as a manifestation of its ideal in relationships to Creative Forces
or God—or the God-Self.

Hence the premise is that while there are urges, these are merely
signs, indications of what the entity has done about what it has set as
its ideal; these do not force the entity to be or to do this or that, but
they have their INFLUENCE! and it depends upon the will or the choice
of the entity, as to whether such an influence becomes constructive or
destructive in the experience. Such urges, as we find, arise from the
varied sojourns in the earth as well as sojourns in the astrological aspects between the earthly sojourns—or during the interims when the
entity is in such an environment as accredited to the astrological aspects
because of their relative position not only to the earth but to the ruling
influence or force within our own solar system or in its astrological
aspect to the whole—or to the Sun, the ruling power or force.

Hence the entity is continuously meeting its own self and what it
has done towards its ideal. And there is constantly the choice before
the mental self (for the Mind is the Builder) as to what it will do with
its opportunities of every nature in its relationships to its ideal in the
activities towards others.

Reading 1650-1

What, then, is the purpose of the entering of a soul into material
manifestations?

In the beginnings, or in the activities in which the soul manifested
individually, it was for the purpose of becoming as a companion of Cre-

ative Force or God; or becoming the whole body of God itself, with the
ability—even as thy Pattern, as thy Savior, as thy Guide and Guard—to
know thyself to BE thyself, yet one with Him!
That is the purpose for each entering into the material activities.

Reading 1754-1

Yes, we have the records of the entity now called [1754].

In giving the interpretations of the records as we find them, these
are chosen from the records with the desire to make the knowledge and
the experience one that may be helpful and hopeful.

These, as will be seen, are rather of an unusual nature.

The entity is such an extremist in a manner; and with the abilities
to make for those experiences in which this sojourn may be a GLO-
RIOUS one—either materially or socially, or in those efforts to become
a channel through which a great many blessings may come to many.

The choice as to which course is to be taken must rest with this body.
It will NOT do both—be a social success and attain material things in
a great measure, and be a spiritual channel for creative forces or God's
purpose to manifest through the experience . . .

Hence, this counsel might be given in respect to same:

Turn rather within. Know that whatever experience ye have in the
material sojourns for a purpose. Know that it is not by chance that ye
are in a material or earthly consciousness in the present. For know
that all activities of the mind, of the body, must be based upon SPIR-
ITUAL things. This does not mean goody-goody, but the PURPOSE,
the ideal—unless it is founded in that which is constructive, which
is CREATIVE, this experience may become—under these extremes—a
torment throughout.

Yet if thy ideals, if thy purposes, if thy desires are set in that which
IS creative, we may make a glorious experience of this sojourn in this
material plane . . .

And it is according to thy own choice as to whether these are constantly constructive, creative, or for the satisfying of material appetites.

For know, it is ever as He hath given—Today, NOW, there is set before
thee good and evil, life and death,—Choose thou!

It is through that factor of Will, then, that the Choice is made—according to thine own Ideal.

WHAT IS thy ideal? in spirit, in mind, in body?

What is thy ideal relationship to thy home, to thy father, to thy mother, to thy friends? Are these creative? Are these in keeping with that which is the messenger of thy own life—thy Mind?

Has not rather the lack of thy choice brought into thy experience, because these were not considered, that disturbing force which arises within thy experience in the present?

Do two wrongs make ANYTHING right? Have ye lived, will ye and do ye live day by day as ye would that men should do to you, do ye even so to them?

This is the law, this is the IDEAL. Not merely idealistic, but the Way of Life!

And as in thine abilities, in thine INNATE desire,—NONE may be more beautiful in purpose, in the life, in the ability to GIVE to others joy, peace, contentment—with all the attributes of the earthly things combined,—passion, with all of its material loves, all of its material desires. These ye know well; but unless these be tempered with thine ideal, thy WILL may lead thee in the paths that become troublesome, dark and disagreeable!

Know, then—He, thy Lord, thy God, thy Christ, is in that position—"If ye will be my child, I will be thy God" . . . Let no day then pass that ye do not speak a CHEERY and an encouraging word to someone! And ye will find thine own heart uplifted, thine own life opened, thy love appreciated, thy purposes understood!

Reading 1909-1

. . . Call more oft on that self from within, for God is not a respecter of persons, as man sees, but everywhere—at every time—calls on all to repent. Give self in that manner, knowing that the body is the temple of the living God, and to present self as a LIVING sacrifice is but a REASONABLE service. Be ready at all times to answer for the faith that is held within, knowing that—as that is committed unto Him—He is able to KEEP that committed against any condition that may arise in self. Avoid the APPEARANCES of evil. Speak not unkindly of ANY man, knowing he is a portion of the same as thine self. God is not willing that ANY should perish, but man's own will makes him one with or turns his face from Him. Keep thine OWN power within thine own hands, and do not ever attempt to tell GOD HOW to do a thing—for His power is sufficient, even in thee!

Reading 1947-3

As was indicated, the body was first a cell by the union of desire that brought activity in that influence about which the growth began.

Then of itself at birth into materiality the consciousness gradually awoke to the influences about same of body, mind and soul, until it reached the consciousness of the ability for the reproduction within itself of desire, hope, fear.

And the whole of creation, then, is bound in the consciousness of self. That influence, that force is the psychic self . . .

What is the purpose of entering consciousness? That each phase of body, mind and soul may be to the glory of that Creative Force in which it moves and has its being.

And when this influence, this growing self becomes such, or so self-centered, as to lose sight of that desire, purpose, aim to be TO the glory of its source, and seeks rather FOR self, then it errs in its application of the influences within its abilities for the application of mind within its own experience . . .

Then, as has been said: There is before thee this day life and death, good and evil. These are the ever present warring influences within materiality.

What then, ye ask, is this entity to do about, to do with, this ability of its own spiritual or psychic development; that may be made creative or may bring creative or destructive forces within the experiences of others?

"My Spirit beareth witness with thy spirit as to whether ye be the children of God or not." This becomes, then, that force, that influence for comparisons; as the entity meditates upon its own emotions, its own influences, these become very apparent within itself for comparisons.

Do they bespeak of kindness, gentleness, patience,—that threshold upon which godliness appears?

Desire may be godly or ungodly, dependent upon the purpose, the aim, the emotions aroused.

Does it bring, then, self-abstinence? or does it bring self-desire?

Does it bring love? Does it bring longsuffering? Is it gentle? Is it kind?

Then, these be the judgments upon which the entity uses those influences upon the lives of others.

Does it relieve suffering, as the abilities of the entity grow? Does it relieve the mental anguish, the mental disturbances which arise? Does it bring also healing—of body, of mind, to the individual? Is it healed for constructive force, or for that as will bring pain, sorrow, hate and fear into the experience of others?

These be the judgments upon which the entity makes its choices, as it guides, directs or gives counsel to those who are seeking—seeking—What? That Light—which has become, which is, which ever was the light of the world!

Reading 2067–3

(Q) Is the prediction true that I will die suddenly at the age of 80 in Tibet?

(A) If you go to Tibet and live to be eighty, you may die there! This depends upon many, many, MANY circumstances. You'll not die in Tibet unless you go there; and there's not the prospect now of going there!

(Q) What ailment or disease will cause my death?

(A) Depends upon what you do about the condition that exists now! As just indicated, it might be arthritis! It might be a long lingering condition from the general effect produced as to heart, or it may arise from a kidney trouble. ELIMINATE these, and then we will find the body will be able to renew itself to be more useful in the physical, mental and spiritual.

Reading 2113–1

As to what the entity's relationships are to be with such through this experience will depend upon the application of the will. Know, there is no urge—astrologically, nor from the sojourns in the earth, either from the past or present—that surpasses the WILL of an individual!

Thus it is given that man makes or fits his own destiny, dependent upon that chosen as his ideal. For, the will is the birthright of every soul from its Maker. Making that will (or applying it) in the constructive, creative direction emanating from the spiritual impulse or desire for good, brings an entity, a soul, into that realm of awareness of God's creative force being present in its relationships, its dealings with others.

For, as has been indicated, and as will be the experience of the entity—inasmuch as ye do it unto the least of thy brethren, ye do it unto thy Maker, thy will, thy birthright, thy God.

These are not merely sayings, but principles, the basis upon which choices by the entity are to be made in its experiences and sojourn during this particular period of consciousness in a material world.

Reading 2462-2

For, it is never by chance that a soul enters any material experience; rather by choice. For, the will is the birthright, the manifested right of every soul. It is the gift of the Creator, yet it is the price one pays for material expression.

Hence the life must be a purposeful one, with a purposeful experience and expression in its relationships. For, some laws are ever in evidence in the experience of those who take thought.

True, by taking thought there may be little added to the material, but the MIND is the builder. Hence the building in a purposeful manner becomes a manifested activity in any material experience, according to the spirit with which it is purposed through the will of the entity.

Thus with this entity the choices have been made through varied experiences in the earth, as well as the astrological sojourns. For, to be sure, each soul manifests in other dimensions through sojourns in the environs about the earth . . .

For, as each soul finds itself body, mind and soul, these express or manifest in the various spheres of experience of an individual entity.

Thus as that manifestation is made active, there is the development or retardment; dependent then upon the choice made by an entity; not in a group, not as a separate force, but as self—whether in tune with divine laws, laws of growth, or laws of material gratification.

Hence the influences of choice may surpass even the experiences that have been a part of the entity through any astrological or earthly-material sojourn.

Reading 2549-1

For, know that each soul is a free-willed individual, and chooses the way and the application. For it is either the co-worker with God in creation—and creative then in its attitude, in its thought, in its application of tenets and truths day by day; OR in attune with that which is at variance, and thus besetting or putting stumblingblocks in the way of others along the way.

Each soul must choose of itself whom it will serve,—self, the glorifying of same, fame or fortune as partakes of material things, or that which is set in the Ideal . . .

Reading 2982-4

. . . For, God Himself forces no individual to seek Him, save by the natural law. It must be free will, that which was given as the birthright to man, as that which the entity here has applied, may apply; the true law of love, not of self, but of Him who giveth all things to all men. For it is not of self but by the grace, by the mercy, by the love of and for the fellow man; not that self must be or even may be exalted in name, in place, in position. For He thought it not robbery to make Himself equal with God, yet came from God's presence that others, His brethren might know; that His activities would offer for man the way.

So in the use of thy abilities in ministering to others as ye may in word, in deed, in humbleness, know it is not of self but as the gift from the Father. For He having first loved us, what manner of man should ye be that ye should use, not abuse; ye should apply not as in the way of honor, or of claiming honor. For who would be the greatest? Ye who will be the servant of all may be the greater among thy fellow man.

Reading 5749-14

HLC: You will have before you the enquiring mind of the entity, Thomas Sugrue, present in this room, and certain of the problems which confront him in composing the manuscript of THERE IS A RIVER. The entity is now ready to describe the philosophical concepts which have been given through this source, and wishes to parallel and align them with known religious tenets, especially those of Christian theology. The entity does not wish to set forth a system of thought, nor imply that all questions of a philosophical nature can be answered through this source—the limitations of the finite mind prevent this. But the entity wishes to answer those questions which will naturally arise in the mind of the reader, and many of the questions which are being asked by all people in the world today. Therefore the entity presents certain problems and questions, which you will answer as befits the entity's understanding and the task of interpretation before him.

EC: Yes, we have the enquiring mind, Thomas Sugrue, and those problems, those questions that arise in the mind of the entity at this period. Ready for questions.

(Q) *The first problem concerns the reason for creation. Should this be given as God's desire to experience Himself, God's desire for companionship, God's desire for expression, or in some other way?*

(A) God's desire for companionship and expression.

(Q) *The second problem concerns that which is variously called evil, darkness, negation, sin. Should it be said that this condition existed as a necessary element of creation, and the soul, given free will, found itself with the power to indulge in it, or lose itself in it? Or should it be said that this is a condition created by the activity of the soul itself? Should it be described, in either case, as a state of consciousness, a gradual lack of awareness of self and self's relation to God?*

(A) It is the free will and its losing itself in its relationship to God.

(Q) *The third problem has to do with the fall of man. Should this be described as something which was inevitable in the destiny of souls, or something which God did not desire, but which He did not prevent once He had given free will? The problem here is to reconcile the omniscience of God and His knowledge of all things with the free will of the soul and the soul's fall from grace.*

(A) He did not prevent, once having given free will. For, He made the individual entities or souls in the beginning. For, the beginnings of sin, of course, were in seeking expression of themselves outside of the plan or the way in which God had expressed same. Thus it was the individual, see? Having given free will, then—though having the foreknowledge, though being omnipotent and omnipresent—it is only when the soul that is a portion of God CHOOSES that God knows the end thereof.

(Q) *Are there several patterns which a soul might take on, depending on what phase of development it wished to work upon—i.e., could a soul choose to be one of several personalities, any of which would fit its individuality?*

(A) Correct.

(Q) *Is the average fulfillment of the soul's expectation more or less than fifty percent?*

(A) It's a continuous advancement, so it is more than fifty percent.

(Q) *Are hereditary, environment and will equal factors in aiding or retarding the entity's development?*

(A) Will is the greater factor, for it may overcome any or all of the others; provided that will is made one with the pattern, see? For, no influence of heredity, environment or what not, surpasses the will; else why would there have been that pattern shown in which the individual soul, no matter how far astray it may have gone, may enter with Him into the holy of holies?

3

●

The Akashic Records and
Influences from Previous Lives

[Note: the following extracts taken from individual Life readings demonstrate how the Akashic Records of the past have a motivational influence upon the present and the unfolding future.]

Reading 169–1   M 21 (Student)

In the appearances, and the effect, the urges gained from same:

In the one before this we find in the land now known as Gennesaret. The entity then was among those that were keepers of the flocks in the fields when the peoples were disturbed by the raids from the Roman rule. The entity gained through this experience, in the name Guidia, for the entity defended a principle and gave to the peoples the better understanding of relationships to those that were in power and those in service. As the effort then is in the present experience towards relationships of the same NATURE, the entity may apply self and will's forces in a CORRECT manner that will bring to self a greater development in the present experience; for these relations govern that of law and of application of penal as well as moral law.

In the one before this we find in the days when there were changes being made in the land now known as Persia. The entity then was among those in power in the land when same was overrun by the peoples from now southern Arabia, and from the north, and the entity lost through this experience; for while in power NOT the good ruler, while in servitude not the good servant; for the entity finds in self in the present experience the hardship of taking orders from any; yet, as is given and as has been seen from that given, to learn to understand self and self's relation is the first law of knowledge, and the application will be that to be served is to be a good servant.

In the one before this we find in that period when there was the reconstruction of the division in the land now known as Egypt. The entity then was among those that came in from the north country, and was the younger son of the king who set up the new rule in the land, bringing much to the peoples in gaining the understanding of that taught by those that were put in power, and by the division the entity then GAINED much in the way of being able to discuss or to understand many sides of a question. This is an urge in the present, as the desire to know more. This is one urge that especially should be developed in the present experience—know both sides of any question, any thing, pertaining to WHATEVER the entity may put self in its entirety—understand the whole!

In the abilities of the entity as seen in the present, these would relate particularly to PEOPLE and to things, whether of lands or of study of any nature as pertains to law, land, or peoples—and in EITHER of these would the entity make the greater success in the financial ways and manners; yet for the greater development keep first the understanding of self and self's relationship to others first and foremost . . .

Reading 187-1   M 5 months

In the one before this we find in the days when the strife was between the peoples in the present land, the entity then being among those who fought in that rebellion. In the name then we find of Artemus Davees [?]. In this we find the urge as will be in that of the thought as is exercised in self, being strong-minded, very centered in thought and action. Hence the necessity as will be of the training of the direction of the mind and of the developing in same.

In the one before this we find in the days of the development of the country into that of the republic forces in France, when the rebellions were in the land. The entity then in that of Vasi Borgenes [?]. The entity then the one that assisted in the capture of those forts about which the soldiers of the ones defending the royalty became the ones necessary to overcome or overthrow these conditions. The entity from this we find gains that dislike for those who would be over-bearing, or those who would be presumptuous in their action. Hence the necessity of those training and giving the correction for the development of the entity of always knowing and showing the reason, and reasoning with the individual in its development.

In the one before this we find in the days of the rebellions in the plains country, when this had become settled. The entity then was in that of the Viva [?] who became the heralder of the new religious thought as was given to that people then in Arabian forces. This we find became the developing point of the entity. Hence in this present urge we will find the desire of the study of such, of the religious thought and study as pertaining to psychological and astronomical conditions. Yet for the same reason, by not being directed properly, may be turned into adverse channels.

In the one before this we find in the days of the Atlantis, when the peoples were in that of the higher state of civilization. The entity then was the teacher in the psychological thought and study, especially as that of the transmission of thought through ether. Hence the urge as will be seen in this entity in the studying of those as has been given.

Reading 195–14   M 42   (Realtor, Manufacturer)

Before this we find the entity in that name of Rhoul (?) [Raoul?], in the days of Louis XV in France. The entity then was in that office of second to the cardinal of that day [Andre Hercule De Fleury (1653–1743)?]. The rule, as was seen through the usage of ecclesiastical garments and position to make or bring about the secular and physical conditions, brought the greater distress, the greater distrust to the individual [195]. Hence there was not given the development in the manner as might have been expected, under the position which the entity then occupied (as rule). For the distrust comes at present, giving in this that urge or desire to know more of the impelling force behind each individual with whom the entity may come in contact, yet finding often that the trust as placed was misplaced.

Before that we find the entity was in the days when there was war between the now Arabian forces and the Persian forces, or between the nomads and the king, Croesus, in Persia. [Croesus II?] [7500 B.C.?]

The entity then was in the name of Oujida, who assisted in the storming of the fort wherein the captives were being held. The entity then was in the warrior and the second in command to the leader [Bedouin] of that day. With the death of the leader, we find the entity fought with the next ruler, or leader, or chief, for the position of lead. Hence the backfire, or rule, as it were; for the company fell out among themselves, and this brought the destructive forces to the entity. The urges as we see from this being that of the tenacity, the 'stick-to-it-iveness.' Though little may be said, there is the ability to follow out, to keep the ends together, as it were, of every condition; and the ability to plan. Also there is exhibited the manner of sleep that is often seen or exemplified in the present from that sojourn. [Gladys Davis' note: He told me that he does sleep like an Arab, on his stomach with his face buried under his arm, as they do in the desert.]

. . . Before that we find the entity during the first of the appearances of man in the earth's plane, during that period when the five appeared. The entity then was in that now of the Nevada and Utah territory in America, then in the name Udulj. The entity was among those who first wrought in iron and in ore, being the first to separate these properties into a manner that might be used for the benefit of man. In that day we find the entity becoming great in the land. And through these channels we find in the present the ability to design, to figure out in mathematical manner, to stick to, those conditions that will give the correct answer in the end toward such conditions, towards such developments of mechanical conditions, those pertaining to work with irons, or that which may be wrought with any forms of ores.

Reading 234–1   M 47

Before this, we find in the days of the Crusade, and this entity then lead in that Crusade, or that known as the Holy War in Palestine, and lost its existence then in that land, and was the second in command at that time. In the present we find this personality exhibited in the love of the study of conditions relative to these Crusades made . . .

Before this, we find in the land of Poseida [Atlantis], when Alta was in the height of its civilization. This entity then was in the service of the country in its relation to other countries, and in the present sphere we find the desire for similar relations ever in the inmost soul of this present entity.

Reading 757–8   F 46

Before this the entity was in what is now known as the north-western or central portion of the entity's present native land—or about Ft. Dearborn [Chicago], during those periods of the internal turmoil and strife—when there were the accumulations of the seven nations to make for the ridding of the country of those that to those peoples were oppressing and overrunning the land.

The entity then was with or in those activities within the Fort, in the name then Spooner. In the experience the entity gained, for there were the activities in the entity's sojourn to make for the better relationships in the associations whether for the commercial or mental and spiritual relationships.

Then the entity was particularly interested in those reports from other lands to the west. Hence there became a longing for the sounds of many waters, where there were the dividing of the lands that the entity sought for its own household. Yet when the persecutions and the turmoils came about, the entity—in a very reluctant manner—withdrew from those places of its habitations, and in the retreat (as was given by the entity would come about) suffered in body; yet coming through—as to those that later began the establishments of a settlement along the lower portions of the Ohio, that emptied into, or where it emptied into, the father of waters.

In the present experience from that sojourn we find that travel, records of such, those things that pertain to the activities of individuals where they may be of mental or material help to others through their associations or relations, though they may be to the utmost parts of the earth, become of special interest. Hence, as indicated from the astrological sojourns, the entity is a mathematically-minded person in the present experience. And also in languages and history; hence teaching in these directions may have been—and may be—a portion of the entity's activity through this present sojourn.

Before that (among those that we find active in the entity's experience in the present) the entity was during those periods of the seeking of the peoples in the English land for the turmoils that were brought about through the activities in the Holy War, or the Crusade activities.

The entity then suffered in body from apparent neglect, as would be called in the present, by those of its own household and surroundings—by being left alone. Hence we find in the present the desire ever for periods to be sure of aloneness, or to draw self—as it were—away; yet in the hours of darkness, in those periods of special occasions, in those periods when there are the happenings for certain celebrations or activity, there is the desire of crowds—or certain associations. And the entity seeks to choose such companions; for innately is there seen from those meditative influences that for certain periods or certain occasions the entity desires NOT the same individual surroundings or associations. The name, Lorna O'Doon.

Before that the entity was in that land now known as the Persian or Arabian, during those periods when there were the buildings of the city in the hills, in the plains, by the teacher that had gathered many peoples from many sources—yea, from many lands.

The entity then was among those from the Persian land that had been under or had seen some of the turmoils and strifes from the associations of Uhjltd. And the entity came as one seeking for not only word of those that had been carried away captive from those raids, but for the bodily satisfaction of knowing that which had—as it were—turned the heads of all the world towards seeking out that lonely nomad.

In the experience the entity then was one of the household, or the wife—or among the wives of the house of the RULER of the land, in the name Tashmia. And the entity was in a position of pomp, in finery, as would be interpreted in the present. While it partook of the things that satisfied for the body, that made for the exalting of the desires of the material surroundings and associations, coming under the influences of the teacher and those activities in the plains and hills the entity sought to turn self in those activities also. And coming again to its own peoples set much in motion that was an aid; returning in the latter days for a sojourn in the city in the edge of the hills; gaining throughout the experience.

And in the present does the entity find, with its applications of those abilities in the teachings of methods and the teachings of ways, in the teaching of the activities, a satisfaction that answers for that something which arises from within from that particular earthly sojourn. Those things in the material world of plaids, the weavings of an intricate and delicate nature, the things that bespeak of the Persian finery—as it may be termed, in filigree—the workings of gold in cloth and such, become as an innate thing; yet finding expressions in the activity oft of the entity in the present sojourn.

Before that we find the entity was in that land now known as the Egyptian, during those periods when there were many of those peoples that were journeying to that land for the reconstructions with the return of the Priest and the incomings of peoples from the varied lands . . .

As to the abilities of the entity in the present and that to which it may attain, and how:

Apply self, then, in those things that make for the finding of self—as to what it uses as its own measuring stick of sincerity, of a standard of living. Then give to others in EVERY way, by precept, by example, by letters, by articles that may be prepared; making its contribution to the mental and mathematicalminded individuals that seek THROUGH such sources for an understanding.

Reading 2449-1   M 60   (Salesman)

Before this the entity was in the land of the present nativity; during those periods following the reconstruction after the American Revolution.

The entity then was a teacher, an instructor, first in the schools and later as a teacher, a writer of the history of the land; in the name then Goodrich.

In the experience the entity gained, though in the material things there was the lack of the forethought to make or maintain the hold upon the results of the efforts in material things, and there was never the equaling of that needed in relationships with others. And the entity was condemned by others for such lack of forethought. Yet, little is brought into the material experience—little may be taken away, save as the assurance of peace or harmony in relationships to thy fellow man.

Before that the entity was active in the earth during the early days of the church, when the activities of Constantine brought purposeful desires on the part of individuals to supply, hunt out, find, those records as made by the early disciples of the Master.

The entity was then as one given, or ordered, to produce that as

had been proclaimed by the entity in its gatherings with others in the
Macedonian land, and in portions of Palestine.

Then in the name Contii, the entity lost and gained, lost and gained;
that is, there were periods when the activities were for self–glorification,
self–indulgences. And yet much of that attempted, and gathered by
the entity as records through the experience, has been and is a part of
those things which have brought and do bring hope to the minds and
experiences of many through this day.

Hence we find the entity in the present is in that position where
many, many may be benefited; but it must be done by the entity in
not a desire for self–glorifying in any sense, nor of that justifying in
the material sense for the expressions in same, but rather to the glory
of truth that may indeed point the way to the fellow man; in knowing,
experiencing more and more his relationship to the Creative Forces, or
God, as may be expressed or manifested in his daily associations with
the fellow man.

From that experience, then, we find in the present sojourn there
may well be a period of devoting the entity's abilities to the activities
as an instructor, teacher or edifier in that as might be called FRATER–
NAL insurance; that bears the stamp of approval in the deeper sense of
self, yet brings a surety or assurance in the material things when there
ARE activities that bring about disturbances or discords in the family
experience.

Before that the entity was in the Persian or Arabian land, in the "city
in the hills and the plains."

There the entity was among the Grecians who were sent for the
interpreting or understanding of the activities in that "city in the hills
and the plains."

The entity became that active force that prompted the tempting of
the followers of Uhjltd in that experience, and thus brought to himself
a disturbing influence—as may be experienced even in this sojourn.
For, the undermining manner in which such was presented through the
gatherings of the many ladies or girls was the littleness that eventually
brought disturbing forces to the entity itself.

Then in the name Ecclestes, the entity lost, the entity gained. For,
coming under those influences as brought about the activities when
physical disturbances arose to such a degree in the experience of the

entity, and by and through that accident which brought a breaking of the body–forces to such measures as to become helpless—the HEAL-INGS as wrought CHANGED the entity in its approach to the unseen; and yet very practical and real experiences through that sojourn.

In the present, from that sojourn then, let the entity analyze self to such an extent as to know what is thy ideal,—mentally, spiritually, materially—and Who is the author of those tenets that lead the entity to accept such AS ideals.

And in the same study to show thyself approved unto God; keeping self unspotted from condemnation of others; keeping the way ever FRESH in GROWTH, in knowledge, in wisdom. For, wisdom is that each should seek. Knowledge may become a stumblingstone, but wisdom is the pathway that may lead to the walks with Him.

Reading 1472-1   F 57   (Writer, Radio Broadcaster)

Before this we find the entity was in the land of the present nativity, during those periods of the settlings in the early portions of the land.

It was when there were those being brought into the land for companions, helpmeets to those of the land.

The entity was among those brought hither from the English land, and become in the household of that family which later grew to be in authority, in power, in that Virginian land; or in the household of that family whose name has been changed to what is now called Byrd—then Bayonne [?].

In the experience, as Clementine, the entity's activities were in the assurance of the freedom of actions for the bringing not only of conveniences into the home but into the activities of the neighboring groups roundabout.

And these have left upon the consciousness of the entity such emotions that oft it finds itself bound by convention, bound by that which prevents the full expression.

Yet know in the awareness that ye will find more and more that the TRUTH indeed sets one FREE. NOT to convention, of the material policies or activities, but in SPIRIT AND IN TRUTH!

For God looks upon the purposes, the ideals of the heart, and not upon that which men call convention.

Before that we find the entity was in the Palestine land, during those days when the Master walked in the earth; and when there were the peoples about those activities of not only the birth but His sojourns before and after the return from Egypt—those whom Judy blessed, that labored in the preserving of the records of HIS activities as the Child; the activities of the Wise Men, the Essenes and the groups to which Judy had been the prophetess, the healer, the writer, the recorder—for all of these groups.

And though questioned or scoffed by the Roman rulers and the tax gatherers, and especially those that made for the levying or the providing for those activities for the taxation, the entity gained throughout.

Though the heart and body was often weary from the toils of the day, and the very imprudence—yea, the very selfishness of others for the aggrandizing of their bodies rather than their souls or minds seeking development, the entity grew in grace, in knowledge, in understanding.

And in the present those abilities arise from its desire, from its hopes to put into the word of the DAY, the experience of the day, in all phases of human experience, LESSONS—yea, symbols, yea tenets—that will drive as it were HOME, in those periods when the soul takes thought and counsel with itself, as to whence the experiences of the day are leading—as to whether they are leading to those activities that are the fruits of the spirit of truth and life, or to those that make for selfishness, and the aggrandizement of material appetites without thought of those things that are creative and only make the pure growths within the experience of others.

Hence whether it be in jest, in stories, in song or poem, or whether in skits that may show the home life, the lover—yea, the weary traveler yea the high-minded, and they that think better of themselves than they ought to think—THESE abilities are there. Use them. For He, even as then, will bless thee with His presence in same. And what greater assurance can there be in the experience of any soul than to know that He—yea, the Son of Mary—yea, the Son of the Father, the Maker of heaven and earth, the Giver of all good gifts—will be thy right hand, yea thy heart, thy mind, thy eye, thy heart itself—if ye will hold fast to Him!

Before that we find the entity was in the Egyptian land, during those periods when there were the gatherings of those from the turmoils, from the banishments, and those from the Atlantean land.

The entity then was among those from the lands that were later called the Parthenian lands, or what ye know as the Persian land from which the conquerors then of Egypt had come.

As a Princess from that land the entity came to study the mysteries for the service it might give to those of her own land, the Carpathians or as has been given, the entity was among the FIRST of the pure white from that land to seek from the Priest and those activities in the Temple Beautiful for the purifying of self that she, too, might give to her own not only the tenets but the practical application of that which would bring home in the material experience an ASSURANCE in the separations from the body.

Thus in the abilities of the entity from that experience, as well as those gained throughout those activities, we find in the present: Just meting out day by day those visions, that ye have gained here, that ye have seen in thy experiences, thy sojourns, ye will find that HE the keeper, HE the Creator, will give the increase necessary for the activities in every sphere of thy experience.

For keeping inviolate that thou knowest gives assurance not only in self but in the promises that He will bear thee UP!

If there is kept that purpose in self, there is little need for a return; save as one that may lead the way to those that are still in darkness. [See 1/20/38 report from her in re this incarnation.]

As to the practical application, then:

In the writing, in the song; in the meting it out in the conversation day by day. For YE can only be the sower. GOD giveth the increase!

Faint not at well-doing.

Reading 1493–1   F 64   (Widow, Dental Hygienist)

Before this, then (among those having an influence in the present), we find the entity was in the land of the present nativity; during those early periods when the Dutch—yea, AND the English—settled in this particular portion of the land; and when those great settlements were led by Stuyvesant, and those activities that soon brought changes into the experiences of the peoples in the land—and in the tradings and in the activities and in the inflow of great numbers of peoples.

The entity then was in the household of one very closely associated with that leader, born in the new land or New Amsterdam, and in the name then Jane Ayer.

In the experience the entity gained; for it endeavors were to safe-guard those of the younger generation that became more and more under the influences of impurities brought by the use of the waters during those periods, and the great stress in that early age when dysentery, diarrhea and such things were influencing the child life in that experience. The entity lent great aid to those that would study same.

Hence the entity gained. For, "He that is the greatest among you is the servant of all," or of the more.

Hence the entity saw its own activities—though under hardships, under discouragements—gradually grow to be in the experiences of men those things that were the influences that would bring hope to the mothers, to the fathers of the land during that experience.

In the present those things become of special interest to the entity that have to do with protective interests of any nature in fighting dis-turbing forces; whether it be poverty, sanitation, fevers or whatnot. And its lending of itself in those directions has brought—yea, will bring—in the present now—the greater peace and harmony of any application of itself in material influences.

Before that, we find the entity was in the land now called the Ro-man, in those periods when there were many of the activities that were barbaric—to the minds and to the intuition of peoples in the present; where those individuals because of their political or religious faiths or beliefs or tenets—were pitted against the beasts of the field, or made to fight as one with another.

The entity then was rather in the position where such things and conditions were viewed from afar; being rather of the royal household or close to those in authority.

Hence the entity's rebellion against those destructions, those mate-rial sufferings, brought into the lives of those that differed from those within power those things that became rather a hardship materially; but a great feeling of those things accomplished in the attempts—in the feebler way in the beginning to put away such barbarity from the lives and experiences of those during those periods.

The name then was Adolpho, and the entity gained and lost, and gained—only when those aids that came to the entity from its losing fights or losing activities in the interest of those peoples oppressed from foreign lands, or those that had been active in other lands and had come under the influence of the teachings of the lowly Nazarene—though persecuted were the peoples for these very forces—was there given strength and encouragement to the entity to carry on.

The entity had many associations during that experience with those with whom it has come in contact, in one way or another, during this present experience. Some have been very lovely, very helpful; some have brought opportunities for activity on the part of the self as well as upon the friend or the associate or the acquaintance for the ridding of many of the disturbing forces.

Hence the entity has known in these experiences many fears and doubts from those that were in authority in political as well as religious places in its experience.

Before that, we find the entity was in what is now known as the Persian land, during those periods of Artaxerxes or Ahasuerus—as he is known by both names; Xerxes from the Grecian, Ahasuerus from the Jewish AND Persian records.

The entity then was among those peoples close unto that deposed queen, and came to know the activities of the peoples; not only of the Jewish, not only of its own lands, but of the many activities that brought the attempt through the king and those co-patriots and co-associates of the entity for the entertainings of the interest in many lands.

Hence the entity knew much of that which was called authoritative; as to rote, as to custom, as to society, as to activities for political and economic reasons or purposes.

Hence those things of particular nature having to do with Persian patterns—yea, those things having to do with the colors of that country or land—have been and are a portion of the entity's consciousness or experience.

Anything of fine linen, anything of brocades, anything of those particular fields of service or activity are of particular interest; though they may be far from the entity's OWN application in same.

The interests in these arises from the activities of the entity in that period. There the entity knew again the vileness of the person, the disregarding of the rights of others; and there was imbued within the mind of the entity, in the heart and soul and purpose, the desire to assist the peoples in freeing themselves through the understanding and the relationships of the spiritual laws of the bondage of self-indulgence.

And these activities become a part of the entity's experiences in the present.

The name then was Eulea.

In the experience the entity gained through the greater portion, and yet many of these things may arise in the present experience to disturb or to cause qualms, as it were, in the mind and the experience of the entity.

Before that, we find the entity was in the Egyptian land, when there were those activities being sent out from those peoples as combined with a uniting of the Egyptians with the Atlanteans; and the teachings that had been gathered from the many places for the considering of interests of every nature were given into the experience of the children of men during those periods.

Such teachings were correlated and disseminated; whether pertaining to the arts, those things of a commercial nature, the delvings into the earth and into the strange places for those things that might be turned into adornments as of silver and gold or precious stones—diamonds, emeralds, onyx, beryl, jasper, and all those things that made for adornment. These were the interests, these were the activities of the entity as related especially to the preparation of individuals for their material actions in those periods.

Hence we find again the entity coming to those influences that become of a special nature in preservation of body, of those things that have to do with the cleansing of same, those that would have to do with individual portions of the body; as the teeth, the eyes, the hearing; as for protection of the feet from activities of different natures; as for dress or for garments or the various characters pertaining to same; or as for those things that may be said to be the hygiene of the bodily forces themselves.

These become interests of the entity in its active associations with its fellowman.

Reading 1549-1   F 55   (Housekeeper, Widow)

Before this we find the entity was in the land of the present nativity, during those periods when there were the settlings in the land by the peoples who sought the ability or the freedom to worship the Creative

Forces, or their religious convictions, according to the dictates of their own conscience.

The entity then was brought up in the early portion of that experience, and in the name then Agatha Charlene.

In the experience the entity gained, because of the abilities to apply self in those directions as a teacher, in ministering to the needs of the home in every way and manner that brought in the experience constructive and helpful forces throughout.

From the abilities and experiences gained in that particular sojourn we find in the present the abilities as a leader, as one who might teach, preach, minister, write or the like.

Before that we find the activities were in the land now known as Palestine, and in the Roman land.

For the entity then was among those who because of the very activities were carried as servants; being a maid, a companion; and BECAME as the leader of the household in the Roman experience, as one who rose to authority.

In that experience the entity gained and lost and gained, then in the name Paulus.

From that experience in the present there are the abilities as a counselor, an arguer, as one who would see the CAUSE of the experiences in the lives of others.

The entity may gain from same the abilities to judge those in authority as well as those that arise from the lay or the common peoples. And these become a part of the entity's experience in the present.

Before that we find the entity was in the Arabian and Persian land, during those experiences when there were those activities in the 'city in the hills and the plains.'

And the influences that arise in the present experience of the entity for the emotions as to the study of the activities of those peoples of the land come from the application of self in the healing arts during that sojourn.

And the abilities as a ministering angel, the abilities for its love and its emotions arise from the experiences of the entity there—as Enderer.

As to the abilities of the entity in the present from same—we find that those experiences of the early associations, as the love affairs, the emotions of the body and mind as respecting home and activities dealing with the various effects of various religious cults or schisms or isms, all become a portion of the entity's experience from that sojourn.

Reading 1562–1   M 44   (Advertising Salesman)

Then, before this we find the entity was in the land of the present nativity, during those periods known now as the American Revolution—and those activities are given that are the main portion of what became the development or adverse, or advancing.

The entity acted as the informer. Not so much what ye would commonly call a spy, but that one who sought out—before the Army, and of the Colonists—as to the abilities of the lands to maintain or sustain those who would be in a manner dependent upon those in that campaign or activity.

Then, as Gordon Weathford, the entity was active in considerations for others. And these oft brought into the experience the lack of the thought of self. This in FACT was development, but this in application in the present may become rather retarding. For because of the lack of appreciation of that accomplished, the entity held grudges; and these do build—as does goodness. The one builds destruction, the other builds hope and glory and patience and brotherly love and kindness and gentleness.

Keep, then, to that thou didst gain there. For as ye sow, so must ye reap.

Keep the faith in Creative Forces.

Before that we find the entity was in the French and the Flemish land, when there were the considerations of those things pertaining to the depicting of the beautiful; to a greater extent even than in the present.

The entity then was associated with those who were of both the schools of the early Renaissance, and brought to self as well as others the appreciations of the efforts on the part of those who made the depicting of nature, the beauty of the body–beautiful, upon canvas—and the water colors.

Then the name was Aruel Meneaux, and the entity in the mental and spiritual gained, in the material not so much—yet the manifesting of these influences in the present experience may bring to the entity the material gains that were during those periods lacking, as it were.

For the fruits of that ye sow must one time be reaped in thy experience . . .

Then, as to the abilities of the entity in the present, and that to which it may attain, and how:

Study to show thyself approved unto God, a workman not ashamed; rightly divining the words of truth, keeping self unspotted from thy own conscious condemnation.

Thus ye will find grace, mercy, peace and harmony becoming more and more a part of thy experience.

Love others, not merely because they love thee but because it brings harmony and hope into thy own experience.

The fields of activity are as indicated, in the fields of service that mete out what ye would have meted to thee.

Reading 1592-1   F 56   (Actress)

Before this, then, we find the entity was in the land now called the British, or English land.

The entity was among those brought who might be chosen or traded, or to make for the preparations of the homes for the early settlers or colonists in the lands now known as the Virginia and Maryland lands.

The entity was FIRST known as Sarah Willmott, becoming Sarah Randolph in the new land; and rising to a position of prominence in the struggles through the early periods, through the application of the material or physical strength to meet the needs and necessities, as well as giving counsel, and reasoning with the individuals of the day.

It may be said that the entity rose to a position that was enviable, not only in the social way and manner but in the home life, the readings, the undertakings, the encouragements to those who became as entertainers, as musicians, as the first character of the actors in that particular land.

Hence, throughout the present or immediate sojourn, such places as those around Baltimore, Washington, Richmond, Cincinnati, Pittsburgh, become the places of experience for the entity. These draw, rather than the city of its present sojourn. Though activities in the city of the present sojourn have been those in which great undertakings have been a part of the experience, the acclaim in the gatherings in those places indicated has meant the more.

As from that sojourn, we find much of those things that have become a part of the manner in which the entity has chosen not to seek companionship as husband in the present. This has been well, for it has been latent in the experience.

But now, as indicated, comes those periods when it would be well to choose to dwell in London–bury–town (?) [Londonderry?], or in those environs about Surrey, in the English land.

Before that we find the entity was in what is now known as the Holy Land, during those periods when there were the turmoils arising among the peoples owing to the various teachings that came to be a part of the entity's experience.

It was during the turmoils arising from the settlings of the land by the Roman rulers, and the variations between the teachings from the Persian and the Roman and the Egyptian lands, and the native peoples.

The entity was among those who were called the Samaritans, and of that city which later turned a great deal of its activity because of the visit of the Master to the woman at the well.

The entity was among those who in the earlier portion of the experience became imbued with the desire, BY the associates, to be among those from whom the channel was to be chosen THROUGH which there might come the promised seed.

And latent within self through the present experience the entity has held that there is rarely given the proper consideration to the union of individuals for the bringing of the young into the world, or into the experience.

These have at various experiences in the present sojourn been a study, a thought, and the entity has followed closely the teachings of many who have given some of their efforts in the line and ideas of the better preparations for the channels through which the protege or the progeny may come.

These arise from the experiences of the entity in that sojourn. For during the latter portion of the entity's experience in the land did the entity come very close to the teachings, the leaders of the Essenes; coming close to the entity known as Judy in that experience.

Until its latter days the entity did not wed; choosing rather the life of celibacy for the preparations of self to be a teacher; and yet felt in the latter portion as though a great deal had been lost that might have been gained through filial and material love in those periods.

The name then was Maryon, or—as would be interpreted in the

present—Mary, Mayan, or Myra.

These were the experiences then, and the entity will do well to follow much of that in the present which is innate; and to WRITE, to lecture on such in small groups or clubs or the lodge—as to such preparations—would be well.

Reading 1755–3   F 42   (Widow, Salesperson)

Before this we find that the entity was in the land of the present environ, during the early settlings.

There we find that the entity was among those groups who were under the teachings, or the environs and influences, of William Penn; not the former or the first, or even the eccentric ones, or those given to such extremes; but the entity there was a teacher, especially in artistic things pertaining to household, and the attractive things for children and those of the younger generation.

In those activities we find that the entity taught rather by the production of joy in the experience of children, than by the quietude or the long-facedness. Yet that very activity, owing to the tenets of much of that environ, created within the entity that which in the present makes for the tendency to be overpractical, or materially intended; though not what might be called material-minded, before spiritual influences or in preference to the spiritual-minded.

Yet with same there is the joke, the practical joker, the practical activity for the enjoying of both the material things and the spiritual blessings—as it might be said.

Well that these be cultivated, but keep them in that way, that manner, as to bring the creative force ever present in thy relationships with others.

The name then was Maria Solomund. In that experience the entity gained, the entity lost, the entity gained; and in the manifestations in the present are those urges, those activities as indicated.

Before that we find the entity was in the Spanish land, during those periods when there were turmoils, and the early activities of groups in manners that made for the recalling of priests and their activity—in the twelfth century.

The entity came under oppressions, because of the desires of individuals or groups to even enjoy the labors of their own hands. These brought persecutions, mentally and materially, into the experience of the entity.

Thus the entity throughout its sojourn felt as one under subjugation continuously; and sought for, and still innately in the present seeks for, SELF-expression, irrespective of what others may think, say or do.

This is well—yet let not self become overactive in self-expression; for the purpose of the entrance into materiality is that the soul-purpose, the soul-desire, is to be guided and led by that which brings the glory to the Creative Forces.

The name then was Parmele Hugden. In the experience the entity gained spiritually—lost mentally, materially.

In the present from that sojourn we find the desire to oft lose self in labor, in work, in those things that would make self forget the burdens of duty or the burdens of "what will others say and do?"

Before that we find the entity was in the Chaldean land, or portions of what is now Iran and Arabia.

There we find the entity was among those groups who studied, who relied upon, activities from the position of planets, stars, the sun, the moon, the phases of same,—because of their interpretations of the influence of same upon the movements of the sea, as well as the activities that came among peoples.

The entity then was what would be called today a soothsayer, a reader of the affairs of peoples—not so much as the prophetess or seeress, yet not one who dealt only with the mystical things, but the practical things,—as the heat, the sun, the light of the moon in its influence upon animal matter, animal activity, physical activities of individuals.

Hence things of that character in the present find an answering chord within the latent forces of the entity, though—because of its unpopularity among its associates or fellows—this is kept well in the background.

The name then was Imashee.

Reading 2073-2   F 39   (Housewife)

Before this the entity was in the land of its present nativity, but journeying into the land of its present sojourn; during the periods following that known as the American Revolution.

The entity settled in those portions of the land now close to the regions between Philadelphia and the Harrisburg areas.

Hence things pertaining to water, things pertaining to nature and nature's surroundings in the present, and also the helpful influences as brought in that experience through same; yet the attractions of activities of individuals who were a part of that new environ brought some disturbing forces. Yet the abilities as were manifested for the making of homes, the establishing of activities in which there were the greater material as well as mental and spiritual benefits, were the result of the activities of the entity during that particular sojourn.

There we find the entity was in the name Nancy Obcher. In the experience the entity gained. In the present we will find things having to do with the natural resources of lands, as natural conditions that arise from individual environs, become problems as well as conditions through which the entity may find harmonious activities; and these bring into the experience that as indicated of great detail, in which the entity may give or describe in its relationships with others.

Before that the entity was in the Norse land, during those periods when there were the activities of those peoples expanding towards the South land, and then into portions of the land now known as the German and the areas close to the pass between the German and the Italian, or the Adriatic activity. All of these were a portion of the entity's experiences, not only as a dweller in those places but as an explorer and one who expanded those activities.

Hence we find that LANDS are of interest, as to their abilities for production, as well as products of every nature; also that nature itself becomes as a teacher to the entity in the present, as does the awakening of all nature, especially in those periods when there is the "spring in the air," as might be termed.

There are the abilities of the entity to depict this, not only in its mental visions or dreams but in the awakening of good from all forms of contention as may arise in the experience of man, and as to how there are the needs for the return to normalcy in its relationships to Creative Forces, from the earth's activity, bringing harmony into the experience.

Thus may the entity use same as one of those channels, as an outlet for its expressions to others.

The name then was Obchellenor. In the experience the entity gained, the entity lost. Through those periods that the activities were given to the study of nature and its application in the affairs of its fellow men, the entity gained. When there were the activities for power in self, ir-respective of the activities of others, the entity lost.

For, all are one. Would that all souls would gain that concept, "Know that the Lord thy God is ONE!" Each soul is a part of thine own, in Fa-ther–God; hence ye ARE thy brother's keeper.

These the entity visions, these the entity feels; yet to make manifest in the LITTLE things day by day, in its dealings with its fellow men, in sowing the seeds of the spirit of truth, is the manner in which ye manifest patience and thus possess your soul—as in brotherly love, in kindness. As ye show yourself friendly, ye have friends. For with what measure ye mete, it will indeed be measured to thee again. For ye are constantly meeting thyself (as is each soul), in thy experiences with thy fellow men. Thus ye bring into the activity in the earth the joy of the Lord, or the sorrow of the LAW that killeth; for it is the spirit of same that maketh alive.

Reading 2381-1   M 37   (Professor)

Before this, the entity was in the land of the present nativity, but in the eastern portion of the land, in the early settlings, when there were those activities especially in the attempts of the settlers to enter the lands now known as Kentucky, Tennessee and Alabama, from the Carolinas and Virginia.

The entity was among those groups who were finally persuaded, and yet against the entity's own better judgements.

Hence we find those manifestations in the entity's present experi-ence, that when opportunities in relationships to working with or as to associations with others are questioned, the entity doubts its own choices at times.

The name then was Alexandria (or Alex) Cullman. The entity gained, the entity lost, the entity gained.

The entity was an instructor, a teacher; not merely of books but of handicraft, as well as of learning. For, the entity was among those settlers who entered into that portion of the land now known as Boonesboro.

Hence in the present we find that in the Carolina land, or portions of Kentucky and Carolina, will the entity's success gradually come—in the present sojourn.

Before that the entity was in the Grecian–Roman period of experience, when the individuals from Greece were chosen as instructors in the Roman land—for the teaching, in games, in music, in speaking and the like.

The entity was a Grecian, coming into the Roman experience, with those of its own as well as the opposite sex; yet the entity in self desired to be the spokesman of his own group, which brought into the experience the turmoils and strife, not only in relations to the companions and associates of its own land but in relation to the differences that arose between those in authority in the Roman land.

But once gaining favor with those groups among the Romans, the entity made material conditions for others quite unpleasant.

The abilities of instruction that arise in the present are well. The abilities as a director—when temperament and judgement, and the graces and beauties of love are manifested—became excellent. When self is sought to be expressed irrespective, or the excuse of principles without the thought of individuals, these become rather questionable.

The name then was Turtelusen.

Before that the entity was in the Persian land, when there were those activities in the "city in the hills and the plains."

The entity was among the Persians who were gradually taken over in part, yet the entity NEVER was among those who became submissive to, or who joined in the activities in the "city in the hills and the plains," but was one who despised (as would be termed in present terminology) those activities which wrought such an influence during that experience.

For, the entity was of that CULT as would be termed of the capitalistic nature today; hence might made right (in its final analysis).

As a business executive, influences arise in the present from that experience that make the abilities good in the entity—FOR business. For the expansions—let love rule; and we may find that these CAN and may be worked together.

The name then was Excelcen.

Before that the entity was in the Egyptian land, but among the young brought from Atlantis.

In those periods when the turmoils and strifes has been put aside, the entity joined with the activities of those individuals given into special service by their tempering, or tutoring, or being taught through the Temple of Sacrifice and the Temple Beautiful; for, these were as the activities of vocational guidance in that experience.

Thus we find the present abilities of the entity in aiding especially the young, or as a teacher, as an instructor towards those things that make the ways of life and the ways of experience for others in their choice of life.

Hence the first injunction:

Learn in self—and through the analysis of self—what ideals are; spiritually, mentally, materially. Let ALL be prompted by the spiritual import. For, as indicated, this alone finds that which is creative, and ever hopeful, and ever building.

In the fields of service of instruction, in teaching, in handicraft, in games—as an instructor or teacher—these are the fields through which greater service may be rendered, greater contentment may be had.

But learn FIRST to rule and direct self. And let the words of thy mouth, in thy counsel to others, be consistent with the purposes of thy heart and thy daily living.

Reading 2397-1   F 42   (Artist)

Before this the entity was in the Yucatan land, during those periods of the early coming in of those from the western shores—or during the Spanish periods.

There the entity was a priestees to the sun god—who attempted to bring into the experiences of her peoples the closer relationships to those peoples through the abilities of the entity to depict in drawings, in the markings upon the face even of nature, as well as upon the walls, the buildings of the peoples, that as would bring awe—and yet an inspirational awe—to so pattern their lives, their activities, as to be acceptable unto the higher influences that are ever creative in the experiences of individuals.

With the interruption of those activities, through the selfishness of men, there came disappointments, disturbances—yea, even HATE into the experience of the entity.

Much of these the entity is meeting in the present,—yet, through the artistic temperaments of self, there is still the ability to depict nature in the form of murals, or the like, upon walls, upon edifices of man today, in such a manner that there may come the knowledge, the awareness, the appreciation being aroused in the minds and hearts and souls of many today, who in their selfishness, thoughtlessness, their desire for aggrandizement, brought those disturbing and confusing experiences in the entity's activity as Princess Quinta.

And with those channels of authority from the ruling forces, or in governmental channels, in government places,—in such activities may the entity find the outlet for these abilities, these opportunities, in the present sojourn . . .

As to the material field of expression—this should be as the artist; in the ability to depict nature—the hopes, the fears, the doubts—but these, let them ever be hopeful rather than fearful. Look up, life up thy heart, thy mind, thy purposes unto Him; for HE is a present help in time of trouble.

Reading 2409-1   M 47   (Sales Executive)

As to the sojourns in the earth—these find expression through the emotions of the body; though for this entity these have not the influence that the spiritual life and the mental activities have brought into its experience. But these may be indicated as part of the experience, showing why there are certain urges latent and manifested in the present—as indicated in the first principle—and what the entity has done, may do, about such urges—here, now; as to its ideals, as to its hopes, as to its material relationships—and what may be expected as the results in same.

Before this, then, we find the entity's activities were in the land of the present nativity, following those turmoils which made for the scattering of the settlers in the Dearborn area.

The entity was among those who fled not towards safety to the south and the east, but to the lands of the present nativity. THERE the entity grew and builded, in the first the desire to help, then in establishing relationships with the natives; in gentleness, in kindness, in patience; not merely for self-preservation but as an announced purpose and desire. Thus the opportunities were brought to gain the best from THEIR activities, and to give of self in what today would be called educational activities.

Thus we find these apparent in the present experiences of the entity:
If the entity sets out to make certain individuals his friends, few

there be with whom he will not accomplish same,—no matter what their station in life may be!

The entity is a good conversationalist; hence an awfully good listener; condemning few, manifesting interest in others and their problems—especially if pertaining to the home or its environs, or its improvements, or such natures.

The name then was Horace Manley. In the experience the entity gained, as may be indicated—for OTHERS came first, in the entity's principles, its desires, its hopes . . .

Before that the entity was in the Arabian and Persian land, when there were those activities from the "city of gold" as well as from the Indian and the Egyptian lands and the areas traversed; that is, when there was the establishing of trade routes.

The entity was among the nomads who, with those developments of the activities in the "city in the hills" BECAME associated with the leaders of the trade—who are today also associates of the entity.

The trading then was in the household necessities; foods and raiment, and those things pertaining to the activities of various groups in their tradings with those who were in the position to create needs or supply same in other lands.

Hence we find in the present that activities pertaining to such are of especial interest to the entity. In most of the lands through which of the entity travels, or with which it becomes associated, the entity comprehends what that section of the country produces that adds to the constructive forces in the experiences of mankind as a whole . . .

As to the abilities of the entity in the present, then, and that to which it may attain, and how:

The field of greater service, as we have indicated, lies in those things or activities where there is the supplying of commodities that lend to the comfort, the welfare and the education . . .

Remember—in thy relationships to others—the RULE does not alter. Ye are forgiven from on High, as ye forgive others.

Hence that injunction—deal with others as with thyself; for with what measure ye mete it is measured to thee again.

Reading 2522-1   F 19   (Stenographer)

Then the entity was in the English land, in the name Arabella Crunch.

While the entity experienced what some would call hardships of an early settler, yet all were benefited by not only the associations but the acquaintanceship with the activities of the entity—not only from its dealings with those in its own household but from its helpfulness in every form of activity to those about the entity.

So, it may be said that the entity gained throughout that experience.

And the abilities to meet circumstances as they arise will be the outgrowth, as the entity applies itself in this present experience.

Put away doubt of self, or doubt of self's conviction respecting individuals or circumstance or things in the experience from day to day.

Know that while what ye are depends upon what ye have been, if ye live TODAY in and with Him—the Giver of all good and perfect gifts—tomorrow there will be more beauty, more harmony in thy experience.

Before that the entity was in the French land, during those periods of the early Crusades—when there were those gathering for a purposefulness in the service and activity in the Holy Land.

The entity was then in the opposite sex from the present, and was active in organized leadership that led many of the peoples of its own land to the Mesopotamian land—where disappointments, yet lessons of truth were gained.

Then in the name Charveliehr, the entity gained, the entity lost. In the present the entity will find those needs for being sure within as to its ideals, in its spiritual, mental and material relationships—and to be SURE, and sure of the sureness in its choice; and then go ahead. Don't wait!

Reading 5260-1   F 50   (Sales Personnel Manager)

That there are more virtues than evil is indicated in the present entity. For there has been growth towards righteous understanding, even with the trials through which the entity has passed from period to period.

As we find, these are as consciousnesses, when the parallel is drawn, or the composite of the experiences of this entity in the earth and of interims in between:

This is an individual entity who is admired and liked by young and old. There is that consciousness such that the entity goes out of its way to be kind and helpful, especially to the young. Not that the entity hasn't a temper, yet the entity does control same very well.

For, as has been indicated, he or she who hasn't a temper is in a much worse plight.

So, in the application, there are abilities in those directions as of a social helper, a social service activity, Red Cross, as it is implied in its broader sense, and the ability to write, which should not be neglected by the entity.

As an individual who would meet or consult, as one who would hire or prepare people, individuals, for their work in large organizations, or as the head of employment bureau, or head of one who would select help. As an individual, the entity is a good judge, then, of human nature, much more than may be implied from the lists of questions the entity oft may ask individuals. For there are the intuitions, and the entity unbeknown to others invites confidences, but remember in thy judgment of others, "As ye do it unto others, ye do it to thy Maker." And with what measurement ye mete, with what judgment ye pass, so may it be done unto thee. For the law is not mocked, and whatsoever an individual entity sows, so must it reap.

As to the appearances in the earth, these, as we find, are quite varied. While not all would be given here, these indicate the pattern of the entity and in those outlines which might give an insight into the greater possibilities, and thus knowledge alone is not sufficient. The ability to make a practical application of same is necessary, as there would be the constant growth.

As has been indicated the virtues outweigh the vices, but the judgments: beware. Yet, it is in such that ye may make the greater success in the material life.

Before this, we find the entity was in the land of the present nativity. The entity was a sojourner or one who entered or came into the land in the early portion of its teen-age life, from what is now Ohio and those lands. Thus the entity in the experience became the homebuilder.

As the home represents that to which each soul entity hopes to attain, so may it be the emblem of that which the entity may do as an assistant in character building for the young, as well as in advice to those of more mature age. In the name then, Lucille Arnold.

While there were material hardships, yet the entity's application as a teacher, as an interpreter for other races, other groups, brought tolerance as well as patience into the experiences of the entity, and fits or makes it befitting for the entity in its service in social service, as well as a head of individual employment for organizations.

Before that we find the entity was in the French land, when there were those foregatherings of groups for the Crusade periods. Here we find the entity in the opposite sex, and quite active in the ideals of those who set about to offer themselves for helpful influences to a cause and purpose. Outwardly very good, inwardly not the same application to the associations or companions of the entity in that period. In the name then, Aaron Ludwig. In the experience, the entity gained and lost, and yet the activities which make for the ability to be for the hale soul, or hale fellow well met in those activities, arise from those experiences.

4

●

The Akashic Records and Planetary Sojourns in Consciousness

[Note: The Edgar Cayce material suggests that between earthly incarnations souls often experience "sojourns in consciousness." These sojourns are apparently intensely focused "lessons" that expand consciousness in specific areas for soul development. In discussing these consciousness experiences, Cayce suggested that some of the planets in our solar system were symbolic representations of these sojourns. It was not that individual souls literally went to these planets; instead, these planets represented the experiences that the soul encountered.

In addition, the readings also suggest that at the moment of each soul's entrance into the earth, the "universe stood still," giving a symbolic overview of that soul's past in terms of astrology—the planets representing a soul's strengths, weaknesses, even past lives. Although it is not always easy to determine whether the astrological configurations described in the readings are associated with sojourns in consciousness or planetary configurations at the time of birth, the following extracts taken from individual Life readings.]

Reading 900–10   M 29

(Q) *As created by God in the first, are souls perfect, and if so, why any need of development?*

(A) In this we find only the answer in this: The evolution of life as may be understood by the finite mind. In the first cause, or principle, all is perfect. In the creation of soul, we find the portion may become a living soul and equal with the Creator. To reach that position, when separated, must pass through all stages of development, that it may be one with the Creator. As we have is this:

Man. In the beginning, we find the spirit existent in all living force. When such force becomes inanimate in finite forces [it is] called dead; not necessarily losing its usefulness, either to Creator, or created, in material world. In that of creation of man, we find all the elements in a living, moving, world, or an element in itself; yet without that experience as of a first cause, yet endowed with all the various modifications of elements or forces manifested in each. For first there is the spirit, then soul (man we are speaking of), then mind with its various modifications and with its various incentives, with its various ramifications, if you please, and the will the balance in the force that may make all or lose all.

In the developing, then, that the man may be one with the Father, necessary that the soul pass, with its companion the will, through all the various stages of development, until the will is lost in Him and he becomes one with the Father. In the illustration of this, we find in the man as called Jesus. In this: This man, as man, makes the will the will of the Father, then becoming one with the Father and the model for man.

(Q) Does the soul choose the planet to which it goes after each incarnation? If not, what force does?

(A) In the Creation, we find all force relative one with the other, and in the earth's plane that of the flesh. In the developing from plane to plane becomes the ramification, or the condition of the will merited in its existence finding itself through eons of time. In the illustration, or manifestation in this, we find again in the man called Jesus. When the soul reached that development in which it reached earth's plane, it became in the flesh the model, as it had reached through the developments in those spheres, or planets, known in earth's plane, obtaining then One in All. As in Mercury pertaining of Mind. In Mars of Madness. In Earth as of Flesh. In Venus as Love. In Jupiter as Strength. In Saturn as the beginning of earthly woes, that to which all insufficient matter is cast for the beginning. In that of Uranus as of the Psychic. In that of Neptune as of Mystic. In Septimus [Pluto? The seventh planet from earth] as of Consciousness. In Arcturus as of the developing. As to various constellations, and of groups, only these ramifications of the various existences experienced in the various conditions . . .

(Q) *Name the planets in order of the soul's development and give the principal influence of each.*

(A) These have been given. Their influences, their developments may be changed from time to time, according to the individual's will forces, speaking from human viewpoint. This we find again illustrated in this: In this man called Jesus we find at a One-ness with the Father, the Creator, passing through all the various stages of development. In mental perfect, in wrath perfect, in flesh made perfect, in love become perfect, in death become perfect, in psychic become perfect, in mystic become perfect, in consciousness become perfect, in the greater ruling forces becoming perfect, and is as the model, and through the compliance with such laws made perfect, destiny, the pre-destined, the forethought, the will, made perfect . . .

Reading 900-24   M 29

(Q) *Explain how, why, and in what manner, planets influence an individual at birth?*

(A) As the entity is born into the earth's plane, the relation to that planet, or that sphere, from which the spirit entity took its flight, or its position, to enter the earth plane, has the greater influence in the earth's plane. Just as the life lived in the earth's plane directs to what position the spirit entity takes in the sphere.

(Q) *What is meant by "influence of the planets in and about earth's plane is deficient?"*

(A) In this relation, as given, that as has been generally taught in times past, not the existent conditions from the spirit plane.

Reading 3003-1   F 61

Yes, we have the records here of that entity now known as or called [3003].

In giving the interpretations of the records as we find them here, there are many definite activities that are apparent in the entity's experience; many an experience to be chosen from, not only in the sojourns in the realms between manifestations in the earth but also sojourns or experiences in the earth.

These, however, we would choose with the desire and purpose that, applied, this information may become a helpful experience for the entity; enabling the entity to better fulfill those purposes for which it entered this present sojourn.

We would magnify the virtues, we would minimize the faults—as should be the policy of the entity, in it choosing activities for others.

As has been experienced in the mental self, there is as much reason to dwell upon the thought from whence the soul came, as it is upon whence the soul goeth. For, if the soul is eternal, it always has been—if it is always to be. And that is the basis, or the thought of Creative Force, or God.

He ever was, He ever will be. And individuals, as His children, are a part of that consciousness. And it is for that purpose that He came into the earth; that we, as soul-entities, might know ourselves to be ourselves, and yet one with Him; as He, the Master, the Christ, knew Himself to be Himself and yet one with the Father.

Thus the purpose of manifestation in the material plane; that we may apply here a little, there a little, line upon line, precept upon precept, that we may become like Him.

And as the entity has through the experiences seen and aided others in the application of their efforts and their abilities to become more and more aware of their relationships to the Creative Forces or God, so may the entity—as He gave—in patience become ye aware of thy soul.

For, as indicated in the three-dimensional consciousness—the Father, the Son, the Holy Ghost,—time, space and patience—man—body, mind, soul—ALL answer one to another. Hence the first law, "My spirit beareth witness with thy spirit."

These become, then, the first principles in this entity's analyzing of itself and of its activity in the earth.

As indicated in the certain periods, remember—as has been given—it is not because ye were born in May, or on the 4th of May, that such and such happened to thee. For, as a corpuscle in the body of God, ye are free-willed—and thus a co-creator with God. Thus the universe stood still, as it were, that ye might manifest in a certain period that ye had attained by thy activity in the earth. For, as He hath given in all places, TIME must be full. An individual entity's experience must be finished before the entity may either be blotted out or come into full brotherhood with the greater abilities, or the greater applications of self in the creating or finishing of that begun.

From the astrological aspects, or the consciousness or awareness in the realms outside of the physical or earth's source—Mercury, Mars, Venus, Jupiter, all become a part of the consciousness. Thus the high mental ability, the abilities to choose.

And the entity's activity should be editing, preparing the writings of others for consumption by varied groups, or to fulfill an individual purpose to which any group or organization has set itself; or, first of all: "Is it in keeping with what He would have thee present to thy brother?" For, "As ye do it unto the least of these, my children, ye do it unto me," is the second law of a universal nature.

Thus as ye choose material as consumption for the mind, or as ye feed the minds and souls of others, they are to bear fruit of Him who is the way and the truth and the light.

To be sure, as He hath given, not all are ready. For, those that are blind spiritually do not see. But they that have fulfilled, they that are ready, THEY will He lift up. And even as He has given, "And I, IF I be lifted up, will draw all men." So in thine activities and in thy choice of material as may be presented to the children of men (and apply thyself in these directions), ye may draw souls to the knowledge of the living God; that He may make manifest in their consciousness the needs of a sin-sick world.

And no more propitious time has been, for the time draweth near that those who are awakened to the needs of the children of men must make known the love of the Father, the grace, the mercy, the PEACE that comes in being in accord with His way.

Thus in Venus—in beauty, in joy, in awakening to activities—the entity may bring NEW HOPE—yea, a new day to the many.

In Jupiter we find the universal consciousness, the universal brotherhood of man. For, as the entity has conceived, God is not a respecter of persons—as men, but calls EVERYWHERE, "Whosoever will, let him take of the cup, of the water of life," that he, too, may know the truth as was set in Him.

Reading 2857–1   F 5
In entering, we find the entity coming under the influence of Venus,

Mercury, Jupiter and Neptune. In the astrological influences in the astrologic aspects for this entity, we would find these at the present would run near that indicated by the sojourn or influence of the entities experience and applied in the present experience in earth's plane will be modified by the environment for the entity. While the astrologic are innate influences, the will and the influence as may come in the moulding of the life as related to earth's experience are changed by environment. WILL—then the alternating influence in an entities' earthly experience as modified in others by other experiences. Astrologically then we find: one of a loving, sunny disposition—ever being controlled by love and afraid of nothing—save influences as we shall see from experiences in the earth's plane. One in mental abilities through Mercurian influence—that is not of the plodding nature—rather that of the imaginative, but always in definite lines—even as the developing mind shows tendencies toward that of the dancer and the desire for and experiences in same—able to keep step—time—and rhythm in an unusual degree—this from both the Jupiterian and Neptunes influence. Loving to parade, show and especially to bedeck self in unusual apparel—in the influence of these may alternations or development in definite direction be made beneficial to the development of the entity.

In the appearances and the effect same has and will have in the entity's experience—there needs be some care taken as respecting the PHYSICAL in the 9th year—and in the SPRING of that year respecting a TEMPERATURE AND THROAT AFFECTION. Being warned—be FOREARMED and with the accomplishment may the voice be added as one that may be made above a mediocre for the entity's own use and for the enlightenment of others.

In the experience before this, we find in that land known as FRANCE and during the period of the 2nd Charles. The entity then one gifted in the application of the voice, and also as an entertainer in the Dance. For the entity then in the name of CHARLOTTE. In this experience the entity gained in that service rendered to others—through that of bringing the understanding of the use of abilities as service to others—and keeping self—SACRED in body and action. In the present the experiences of that influence are seen—in present thought or intent and the imaginative influence. The entity should live near large bodies of water—and cross large bodies for the better development of the entities abilities.

In the one before this we find in that land now known as GREECE—
the entity then among those that were—what would in this period be
termed models for those that carved in wood and stone and sculptors.
The entity lost and gained through this experience—for beauty of form
turned to destructive influences in the activities of the body during
that experience—gained in the suffering that came in the latter portion
of that experience—and much may be gained—by those in care of the
development—by influences about the entity—from this experience in
influencing, training entity to not regard self's own aggrandizement of
desires in body, mind or activities.

In the name PRYMME. In the present influence in the entity's experience—love of self adornment and of self's own physique.

In the one before this, we find in that land known as Atlantis. The
entity then among those of the people—when the destruction to the
land came—in trying to escape the entity lost in that experience—for
with those who escaped to the land now known as South America the
entity assisted in establishing selfish desires among the peoples who
the entity abode with. In the name OMLU. In the experience in the
present will be the tendency to over ride opinion—and WELL that this
be trained in direction as will be countenanced by authority.

In the abilities of the entity and that to which it may attain in the
present—and how: As seen—much will depend upon the influence and
training—as yet little of the spiritual thought has been entertained by
the entity—the basis of expression in any direction—whether development as the dancer or musician—this portion must not be left [out] in
this experience—for this should ever be the basis of human expression
in the earth's experience—for therein a physical manifested form ALL
influences find expression.

Ready for questions.

(Q) *What period in Greece did she live in?*

(A) In the latter days of Xenophon.

(Q) *From where did the entity take flight to enter into physical form?*

(A) In present—in Venus; In France—in Mercury; In Greece—in Jupiter; In Atlantis from Neptune.

Reading 2144-1   F 41

There are influences, urges latent and manifested in the entity; the entity being body, mind, soul, that which manifests in and out of material, mental and spiritual consciousnesses.

Thus we find urges, owing to that which has been practiced or applied in the various stages of development or retardment, that are measured by what has been called astrological, numerological terms, or by that to which the entity in any phase of its consciousness has attributed or given an urge or influence.

Then, we find there are the varied influences, that are termed by those of varied thought or study, or cult or activity, according to that needed in this or that experience.

Know, however, that no urge, no influence is greater than the birthright of the entity—the will; that which is given to the soul to manifest in the beginning, as to be active within itself, independent of or in coordination with its source, or divinity itself. Yet the very gift of the Maker is divine. But this may be used or abused. It may be applied or laid aside.

Thus we find that the sojourns about the earth, during the interims between earthly sojourns, are called the astrological aspects. Not that an entity may have manifested physically on such planets, but in that consciousness which is the consciousness of that environ. And these have been accredited with certain potential influences in the mental aspect of an entity. We find that these become more and more applicable AS that influence is exercised in any given period of an entity's material experience.

As we find with this entity, there are the influences from sojourns on Venus, Mercury, Uranus, Saturn, Jupiter—about in the order named these have an influence. Thus we find, irrespective of what the entity has done in the present, these are manifested in these manners in the physical, mental or spiritual activity of the entity in the present, and may become MORE of an influence as such application is made to increase their efficacy or efficiency in the experience of the entity.

In Venus we find the nicety of things, of conditions,—the appreciation of influences and forces; yet demure, quiet in its manner, because of the relationships same HAS borne through the application of that very force in other sojourns in the material plane—as will be indicated through the appearances in the earth.

From Mercury we find the high mental ability, the necessity for reasoning things out—within the own mind, that of reaching conclusions by the entity.

Also from Uranus we find the extremes that have been and will be in the experiences of the present sojourn; the interest in the occult or mystic, and the studies of same, and away from that which is called orthodox in every phase of human experience and endeavor. Yet, from Saturn we find the tendency to store within, as well as to make sudden changes without giving thought or credence as to what others would think.

The entity is hemmed in, then, at times, by convention of others, or as to the needs of this or that because of what others will say or do.

Jupiter, making for the benevolent forces in all of these, will bring in the latter portion of the experience—and it should begin within at least the present year—more satisfactory conclusions as to travel, as to unusual scenes,—indicated both in Venus and in Uranus, as well as in Saturn. These should in the latter portion of this present sojourn find material manifestation. For the love of travel is indicated, not only by the astrological but from the material sojourns, as will be seen by the very varied experiences in the material sojourns.

The astrological influences arise as latent forces, or as the dreams or the thoughts of the entity, while the influences from the material sojourns find expression through the emotional or sensory forces of the material body—which ofttimes are confused, especially by those who attempt to study or to materially apply mystical forces. For, the emotions of the body do not wholly correspond to spiritual awakenings.

Reading 909-1   M 62

As to the astrological influence from the sojourn of the entity, we find these are as innate and manifested influences according to the activity of the will in relationship to same. For while one may be under the influence of this or that experience, the will is that factor which makes man different from the rest of the animal kingdom—or that which makes him in the position where he may be lord over creation in a material world, so far as the earth's sojourn is concerned. Yet influences from environs, heredity, and the experiences through which an entity or soul may pass, all have their effect upon that which makes for the entity's abilities in certain directions. It is the choice that makes for that towards its destiny in any given experience, or that commonly called what "the fates hold in store" for an entity. In this entity then, [909], we find:

The sojourn in Jupiter makes for the extremes in its relationships with conditions and individuals. Those of very high and very low estate have been the companionships and associations; those where-unto there might be—from the material standpoint—exceptional op-portunities in many directions; and those that have made for MANY questioning things arising with many of the associations. This influence has made for the peculiarity of the kind and character of friendships that the entity makes; there having been periods when—it might be said—there have been a great many ups and again a great many downs, in the material, the mental and the spiritual outlook of the entity upon that which the activities in a material plane mean in the experience of the entity. Dealings with things that have to do with great value to many individuals as to their relationships; dealings with things having to do with the health or the evaluation of life as an experience in the affairs of others in its relationships to the world. These have and do become a portion of the entity's innate and manifested experience. Their activity depends upon how the entity WILLS, and has willed, to act in relationship to such conditions.

From Mars do we find the adverse and also favorable influences in the experience of the entity; making for times when the entity—it may be said—gained by the inactivity of others, and other times when those in whom the entity had depended have failed—and thus brought adverse conditions and experiences in the associations and activities of the entity.

The influences in Neptune make for interests in activities of individ-uals as to their own prowess, their own abilities in given fields; whether in the political, religious, musical, commercial, or in what form. Espe-cially ADVANCED individuals have been of interest to the entity, and oft in the associations with same—rather than that ordinarily termed which comes from the attributed valuations of indwelling in Neptune influence (of water); yet rather water has played, does and WILL always play, an important part in the material activities of the entity, rather than its life or sojourn near or upon water; and brings also some of those periods when there have been accidents in or near water, or near accidents that have been a portion of the entity's experience.

Reading 3744–4;   Questions on Astrology

(Q) Please give a definition of the word astrology.

(A) That position in space about our own earth that is under the control of the forces that are within the sphere of that control, and all other spheres without that control. That is astrology, the study of those conditions. In the beginning, our own plane, the Earth, was set in motion. The planning of other planets began the ruling of the destiny of all matters as created, just as the division of waters was ruled and is ruled by the Moon in its path about the earth; just so as the higher creation as it begun is ruled by its action in conjunction with the planets about the earth. The strongest force used in the destiny of man is the Sun first, then the closer planets to the earth, or those that are coming to ascension at the time of the birth of the individual, BUT LET IT BE UNDERSTOOD HERE, NO ACTION OF ANY PLANET OR THE PHASES OF THE SUN, THE MOON OR ANY OF THE HEAVENLY BODIES SUR-PASS THE RULE OF MAN'S WILL POWER, THE power given by the Creator of man, in the beginning, when he became a living soul, with the power of choosing for himself. The inclinations of man are ruled by the planets under which he is born, for the destiny of man lies within the sphere or scope of the planets.

(Q) Do the planets have an effect on the life of every individual born?

(A) They have. Just as this earth's forces were set in motion, and about it, those forces that govern the elements, elementary so, of the earth's sphere or plane, and as each comes under the influence of those conditions, the influence is to the individual without regards to the will, which is the developing factor of man, in which such is expressed through the breath of the Creator, and as one's plane of existence is lived out from one sphere to another they come under the influence of those to which it passes from time to time.

In the sphere of many of the planets within the same solar system, we find they are banished to certain conditions in developing about the spheres from which they pass, and again and again and again return from one to another until they are prepared to meet the everlasting Creator of our entire Universe, of which our system is only a very small part. Be not dismayed [deceived]; God is not mocked; "Whatsoever a man soweth that shall he also reap." [Gal. 6:7]

In the various spheres, then, through which he must pass to attain that which will fit him for the conditions to enter in, and become a part of that Creator, just as an individual is a part of the creation now. In this manner we see there is the influence of the planets upon an individual, for all must come under that influence, though one may pass from one plane to another without going through all stages of the condition, for only upon the earth plane at present do we find man is flesh and blood, but upon others do we find those of his own making in the preparation of his own development.

As given, "The heavens declare the glory of God, and the firmament sheweth His handyworks. Day unto day uttereth speech, night unto night sheweth knowledge." This from the beginning and unto the end. [Ps. 19:1, 2]

Just in that manner is the way shown how man may escape from all of the fiery darts of the wicked one, for it is self, and selfishness, that would damn the individual soul unto one or the other of those forces that bring about the change that must be in those that willfully wrong his Maker. It is not that which man does or leaves undone, but rather that indifference toward the creation that makes or loses for the individual entity. Then, let's be up and doing—doing—"be ye doers [of the word], and not hearers only". [Jas. 1:22]

(Q) Give the names of the principal planets, and the influence on the lives of people.

(A) Mercury, Mars, Jupiter, Venus, Saturn, Neptune, Uranus, Septimus. Influence as is given by many of those in and about the earth plane is defective. Many of the forces of each is felt more through the experience, by the entity's sojourn upon those planets than by the life that is lead other than by will, for will is the factor in the mind of man that must be exercised. The influence from any is from what planet that soul and spirit returns to bring the force to the earth individual, as it is breathed into the body, from whence did it come? that being the influence. Not the revolution of the ideas as given from those who study of those forces, but study those that come, as the Star of Bethlehem came to the earth as the individual pointing out the way to Truth, the Light, and others can only be such as prepare their way through that light and influence.

(Q) Are any of the planets [in our solar system], other than the earth, inhabited

by human beings or animal life of any kind?

(A) No.

(Q) Give the description of the planet nearest the earth at the present time, and its effect upon the people.

(A) That planet now fast approaching the earth, under whose influence the earth's minds trend, will be for the next few years, as time is known here, is Mars, who will be only thirty-five million miles away from the earth in 1924. The influence will be felt as this recedes from the earth, and those of that nature; that is, given through sojourn there, express in their lives upon the earth the troublesome times that will arise, only being tempered with that of those who may be, and will be, coming from those of Jupiter, Venus and Uranus, those strong ennobling forces tempered by those of love and strength.

(Q) What effect will the planet, Uranus, have on the people during the next two years?

(A) We find in this planet those of the exceptional forces, those of the ultra forces, those that carry the extremes in every walk of physical life and forces, and these are those that will, in the next two years, especially, give of their strength to the greater force, as has been given. Those, tempered with the forces as received there, find in the tumultuous times that are to arise, the setting ready for their again forces. Well may the earth tremble under that influence in 1925 and 1927.

(Q) Is it proper for us to study the effects of the planets on our lives in order to better understand our tendencies and inclinations, as influenced by the planets?

(A) When studied aright, very, very, very much so. How aright then? In that influence as is seen in the influence of the knowledge already obtained by mortal man. Give more of that into the lives, giving the understanding THAT THE WILL MUST BE THE EVER GUIDING FACTOR TO LEAD MAN ON, EVER UPWARD.

(Q) In what way should astrology be used to help man live better in the present physical plane?

(A) In that which the position of the planets give the tendencies in a given life, without reference to the will. Then let man, the individual, understand how WILL may overcome, for we all must overcome, if we would, in any wise, enter in. Not that the position gives man the transport, but that that force as manifested in the creation of man wherein choice between the good and evil, exercising highest will force, may be manifested the greater in man. DO THAT.

(Q) Who were the first people in the world to use astrology, and what time in history was it first used?

(A) Many, many thousands, thousands of years ago. The first record as is given is as that recorded in Job, who lived before Moses was.

(Q) Are the tendencies of an individual influenced most by the planets nearer the earth at the time of the individual's birth?

(A) At, or from that one whom is at the zenith when the individual is in its place or sphere, or as is seen from that sphere or plane the soul and spirit took its flight in coming to the earth plane. For each plane, in its relation to the other, is just outside, just outside, relativity of force, as we gather them together.

Reading 945-1 F 26

It is well that something be given as to the causes of the records, or as to the houses of records, that the entity may use in a practical application those experiences to aid in making the present experience the more worth while.

For, as a conclusion may be drawn from that in the material plane, the knowledge of any subject, condition, or knowledge of any nature unless put into practical use becomes of little effect in producing in the experience of an individual any activity worth while.

The activities from the astrological standpoint, then, are used as a basis; for the experience of the soul-entity in its activity is continuous. Hence the greater influence, or among the greater influences in the experience of ANY entity, is an indication of the threefold life—or three-fold motivating influence. For there is the material expression (which is of the physical or the earth earthy); there is the mental body, phase or experience of an entity (which partakes of or is an enfoldment or unfoldment of the experiences of the entity in the realms ABOUT the earth—or of which the earth is a portion); and the indwellings of an entity in the interim of its earthly or physical manifestations produce certain activities that make an entity, body or unit act as it does through any given earthly experience. Then, these are of that called the MEN-TAL consciousness of an entity or soul. What have been the motivative forces in the activities of an entity through any given experience, then, or any period of manifestations in these various spheres, may be used as a criterion as to the expressions that may be expected of the entity; as to its reactions, abilities, shortcomings, developments, when SOME or A particular criterion or standard is used.

What then (may be very well asked) is the standard or ideal from which a line may be drawn in such information or for an entity in its development?

That which has been set in Him throughout the ages of this expression of the love of the Creative Force for His creatures.

For man and woman in their manifestations are given—by the All-Wise, All-Merciful Father, the First Cause, the Mother-God, the Father-God—the opportunity to be one with Him. Hence they are given the attributes of the various phases through which the entity or soul may become conscious or aware of that Presence abiding with or withdrawing from its activities; dependent, to be sure, upon how that entity or soul uses the opportunities.

For without the gift of free will to the soul, how COULD it become aware of the Presence of the All-Abiding Creative Force or Energy called God?

Then, as this relates to this individual entity, now called [945], we find the entity born in the present under and in those environs from the astrological aspect of Mercury, Venus, Jupiter, Mars, Saturn.

What meaneth this? That during the interims from the earthly sojourns or experiences the soul has been in the environs that have been given the names of the various planets about or within the solar system of which the earth is a part. Thus the planets have their influence as to the various attributes of that we find expressed or manifested in the earth's environs as what we term as carnal or earthly or three-dimensional forms of awareness.

But what is termed the dimensional environ of the mental capacities expressed by Mercury enables an entity or soul in the earth's environs to give a manifestation of high mental abilities, high mental capacities. Thus we may observe that such an one is enabled to obtain what we call knowledge, as pertaining to mental faculties, much more easily than those whose environs or indwellings previous to the earthly manifestation at present have possibly been in Saturn, Mars, Venus, Uranus, Pluto or the Moon. But what meaneth these? That these abilities are such as termed good or bad. These EXIST as conditions. And it is what a soul or entity does ABOUT such conditions, or what it uses as its standard of judgement, that produces what is called in man's environment Cause and Effect. The same may be said of each of the other spheres or experiences or phases of the indwellings of the entity; in Venus, Mercury, Mars, Jupiter, or all such that have been the experience of the entity, producing those elements within the MENTAL which is of the body or entity a part.

Then, for this entity, we find:

Mercury makes for the high mental abilities.

Venus makes for the emotional side of the body or entity in the present, that becomes at times rather lacking but at others makes for the great motivating influences and forces in the experience of the entity; that it holds as a duty to self, as a duty to its relationships in its various spheres of activity in a material world. For its environs and activities from this association in Venus have made for not sentimentality, but sentiment is a portion; yet as Mercury is the ruling influence this is done from reasoning rather than from sentiment alone. Yet it makes for those experiences in the present within the entity that have at times brought about the appearance or the feeling of a definite loneliness within the entity; the lack of a friend sufficiently close, a companionship sufficiently close to rely wholly upon.

Those are as longings that are being sought within the entity's experience. But as we find, as Jupiter has within the last few months become rather the ruling influence in its sojourners within its environs, as Venus and Mercury and Jupiter are brought more and more into the expression of activity within the experiences of those who have indwelled there, it will bring for this individual entity—in this year or in the next year—a union with such a soul in which the HOME (that is so longed for at times) may be established by the entity. And one whose birthday and associations are near the same year as self's—that is, in 1907-6-5, whose birthday is in the latter portion of June of between that and the 20th to 26th of July—will make for the better companionship with the entity in its experiences.

We find also Saturn having been an influence that has made for experiences within the entity's activities in the present in which it has continued to long for changes in its associations. This has caused the entity at times to find itself dreaming; having day dreams, as it were, by longings for that building up as to itself an ideal relationship or condition that would be—as the entity has visualized—the greater activity in which it might engage itself; either for the satisfying of the material desires or to create the character of environment in which the mental and soul forces might find the greater expression. More often have these considered rather the MATERIAL things. But as these changes have gradually passed, more and more does there come now in the experience that as sought from the mental and the spiritual expression rather than from the purely material.

For the earth and Saturn are opposites, as it were; for to Saturn go those that would renew or begin again, or who have blotted from their experience much that may be set in motion again through other influences and environs that have been a portion of the entity's experience.

In Mars we find there have been periods and experiences when anger, wrath and sudden conditions or certain things in others about the entity have caused changes, or made great changes in what may have been the experience of the entity. These have been rather from without than from within the entity's own associations and environs, but have dealt their influence in the experience of the entity. And these have come within the entity's experience rather as fears that such might arise in the entity's OWN experience; coming again to the reasoning, as it were, from its close Mercurian influence in its own experience in the present.

These, then, are the astrological aspects as we find them from the MENTAL experience that lies INNATE and give expressions in the manner as we have indicated.

Reading 5040-1   F 44

In giving the interpretations as we find of the records here, there are many abilities and many activities of the entity, that would depend upon the ideals and purposes with which entity makes application of the tenets and truths the entity may embrace.

As will be seen from the composite of the astrological and earthly sojourns, there are very unusual characteristics that the entity finds deep within itself; few people fully understand or comprehend the entity, in that the entity feels itself superior, but oft just the opposite, because of this lack of full interpretation or understanding in the experiences. This makes the entity ofttimes very lonely, even with those closer associates about it.

Again we find the entity with the ability such that if it attempts to attract any of the opposite sex, he is already "hog-tied", as far as this entity is concerned, for there are those characteristics and those abilities in the means and manner in which the entity may draw in the sentimental, as well as the deeper feeling of the opposite sex. This can be used, or abused, dependent upon the ideals and purposes.

The entity is indeed a good conversationalist; thus the entity could, if it would apply itself, write well; compose well, and might write stories of deeper morals, and parables, or detective stories. Whatever type of writing is chosen in these directions, the entity will indeed succeed in same.

In giving the urges which arise independently (for these are as a composite, as it were, of the entity's activity in the earth, as well as in the realms of other dimensional consciousness), these we give as astrological aspects: Mercury, Venus and Venus with Mars, with Uranus, with Saturn. Hence the high mental abilities and thinking qualities of the entity, and it, in its thinking, usually remains in the same thought it has reached its own self, and others at times call the entity "hard-headed" or as the entity should find because others are "thick-skinned" or sarcastic in their relationship, it doesn't always mean that they know, or intend to hurt; yet the sensitiveness of the entity, and its ability to attract or to push away others are subject to being ruffled with such conditions, and it has happened and does happen often and plenty!

In Venus we find the abilities to write; we find beauty; loveliness; the ability of making itself lovely; because very rarely would you ever find this lady when she doesn't look well-dressed, even with a Mother Hubbard on!

We find in Uranus the extremes in which the entity has been, or may be put at times. But finding self in its spiritual purposes, spiritual ideals, will make a great deal more tolerance to those who are sarcastic. And as for sarcasm, the entity seldom lets itself go.

Reading 5164-1   F 32

In giving an interpretation of the records as we find them, these we choose with the desire and purpose that this may be a helpful experience for the entity, enabling the entity better to fulfill those purposes for which it entered this present sojourn. We would magnify the virtues, we would minimize the faults. This, we would give, should not be merely the policy but the activity of the entity in itself.

There are those influences that go with the entity such that it can make others do just as it would have them do. This often has caused the confusion in the experience of the entity, and is that about which counsel would be suggested. For, know (not as preaching), all of the good, all of God, all of bad, all of evil that ye may know, is within thine own self. Thus it depends upon what spirit, what purpose, what hope ye entertain as to whether that ye desire to accomplish in thy experience is to be accomplished or not.

As there is a high emotional nature, we find that art, music, things which have to do with entertainment are parts of the consciousness. That ye have at times sacrificed thine own desire to go in these directions, for that which the entity persuaded itself was for the common good of all, was not necessarily the best choice. For whenever there is not the answer from within that, that choice which is made is in accord with that which is best within self, then it becomes disturbing, unsatisfactory, it brings an environ not altogether good. For there is the continual knowledge back in the subconscious of the entity, that greater possibilities could be, would be within the experience if circumstances were different. Know then, this: that ye entered not into this experience by chance, but sought expression from other consciousnesses.

As indicated, Venus, Jupiter, Mercury, Mars are parts of the consciousness. Just as thy activities in choice of physical activity. Ye entertain conditions in certain directions, but music and those things which pertain to same are a part of the soul-entity; and that is eternal.

Then without that there cannot be found the complete expression; whether it is music by instruments, or music by just the fact of doing good, or music by that of just being quiet in the moonlight, or just listening to the night voices. That's music of the soul, and in such ye may wind any fellow around your finger, but for what? That has disturbed the entity.

Let it not disturb but set your mind, set your heart on doing those things; not that just to gratify your own appetites, your own desires, but in doing that in which ye may give more hope, more joy, more pleasure, more activity to others in such a service and ye cannot fail, so long as ye put thy whole trust in Creative Forces or God.

In those things which pertain to the very awareness of being alive should be found the consciousness that there is an opportunity for thee in the present experience.

Then in those fields of entertainment, of music, of art; where hope is given, where there is the desire for greater awareness of creative things, not the sullen things, not those that are of the moment, but the deeper things, may the entity find the outlet for its abilities latent and manifested in the personality and individuality of this entity.

In Mars there is the making for little differences, but an activity. Know deep within self that it is true, you'd better be doing something, even if it's wrong, then doing nothing at all. For the mind is the builder, but in self.

As in Venus, music, activities in entertainment, art, all of these are parts of self.

In Jupiter there is the great activity and desire for a universal consciousness, and this has betrayed thee, as it were, oft by what other people say. But dare to be thyself. For the Lord hath need of thee among many; seeking to represent, to present, to be active in a definite cause.

Reading 1221-1   M 43

In giving the interpretation of these records, the intent and purpose should be for the entity to approach same with the idea, with the ideal of using that which may be helpful in making for soul development.

For only fame or fortune, position or renown, is material; and they that look only for material benefits, or for an easy way, or for an excuse, become as stumblingblocks for themselves.

The purpose of the entrance of each soul is that it may develop towards being as one with, being a companion with Creative Forces or—as commonly called—God. This is the opportunity then in each experience that each soul bears in relationships to those things that offer the opportunity for being a channel, being expression of, toward the fellow man, of that as the entity holds as its relationship to its Creator.

In the astrological, or from those sojourns that are termed astrological, we find one of high mental abilities through the Mercurian, the Martian, the Venus, the Jupiterian and Saturn. All have their influence in the experiences of the entity; each according to the will—and this in the application of that as lies in the abilities of the entity through its sojourns in the earth has used these for woe. These may be used in the present for that as may make amends, as may make for an atonement in the present or an at-onement with Creative Forces. And that should be, that must be that which the entity leaves with each individual for whom, to whom he may give that as is their astrological or astronomical aspects, that have a bearing upon the latent or the material urges of an entity. These are as tests, the urges that arise—and the test is ever that they must be measured by that as is the standard, the ideal of an entity.

For while the mental abilities are high, so is the self importance, so are those influences that make for the entity desiring those urges for position, for fame, for power.

Power in the hands of those that consider not from whom this power arises, this power is given, becomes as a millstone to each and every soul.

So in the application of those abilities, those influences wherein there are the urges for the application of self in these directions, hold fast to an ideal founded not in earthly things, founded not in ONLY mental things but spiritual application of the mental forces, mental abilities, not only of self but in others. And he that is wise considereth the way of the spirit. What be the fruits then of the spirit? What be the motivative forces?

Gentleness, kindness, longsuffering, brotherly love, patience—these be the measuring sticks, these be those influences that must govern each and every activity in the relationships to not only individuals but to opportunities in giving, in aiding, in assisting others that seek for thy understanding.

In those things in Jupiter we find material things coming into the hands of the entity, but let these come aright; let these be the result of efforts—not in advantage of same for self but rather as the result of mercy, of patience, of love shown in thy relationships to others—in the activities of thy hands. For He, the Lord, IS He through whom all increase comes. The greater then the increase, greater thy obligations—not to self but to thy fellow man, to thy being the channel through which the knowledge of truth as is of Him becomes a part of thy message ever to thy fellow man.

Reading 1473-1   F 49

Yes, we have the records here of that entity now known as or called [1473].

What an unusual shape! as if this in itself had much to do with that the entity has had to do with the unifying of thought of those who have sought to interpret the records left by the sages, as ye would call, of old.

This in itself would appear to signify that the entity's application of self in the present will find a greater outlet for itself in seeking the correlation of those tenets and truths left by those in the eons and ages, that have attempted to leave for posterity—or man—a vision of that which prompted the activities of human endeavor throughout the ages.

And as to how they are, as through the solar as well as the years as by the fixed stars, come into the experience of man to bring a new order in the dealings with the elements, and the activities of same as related to the associations of man's endeavor.

Is there little wonder then that television, radio, flying have a DEEP influence? Not so much the act as the influence such has upon the relationships of man as his brother, under the varied climes or varied aspects of the experience.

But to give the interpretations from the records of time and space, or the akashic records, of this entity called [1473] in the present:

Those influences—as the entity experiences—that arise in the relationships to mind as the controlling factor in the experience of a human entity, are correlative and have their relative relationships to the astrological aspects, the numerological influences, as well as those from sojourns of an entity or soul in materiality or in matter.

Hence we find, while these are influences—relative—none of these surpass the will of the individual entity.

For the will is a portion of the soul-entity, a part of—or creation itself. And as every atomic structure of the bodily force is in relationships as one to another, so each soul in its relationships to a universality of activity, of evolution, as of the very movement of itself through time and space, becomes a part of an influence.

Yet will is dominant even of that.

Hence choice and will become the predominant forces; and the urges that arise in the human experience as from this that makes for that which is ruled by the mind, ruled by the influences from the astrological aspects, may allow itself to be influenced, or may influence those in other aspects to a greater or lesser degree, according to their relative relationship from a numerological aspect.

As One is the factor, and every division of same becomes a portion of that unit, so do we find from the astrological aspect the influences from Jupiter, Uranus, Venus, Mars, Saturn, with the effects—for this entity—of the Moon and the Sun.

For Two becomes a factor in the experience of the entity; not as a divided influence but rather the abilities to weigh or compare in the experience of the entity two degrees beyond that of many with whom the entity may find even much in common.

In Jupiter we find influences accredited by astrology as not only protectorate but as disseminating among the masses.

Hence the influences in which the entity may find itself engaged, or the influences that arise from its material activity will affect many—the masses rather than the individuals; though to be sure reaching same through individual application.

From Uranus we find the EXTREME influences. Hence the entity's experiences are those as of just ready to grasp the meaning of much being sought, in the interest of the occult and the spiritual influences and forces; and again to the very depths of "No use—it escapes me!" These then become factors in the experience of the mental forces of the entity, in which there is manifested from the spiritual aspect the Mind—AND Choice, AND Will.

Venus as the friendship or love influence has very unusual aspects, with the aspects of Jupiter, Uranus AND Saturn with Mars. There are very few whom the entity trusts ENTIRELY; yet holding friendship, love, and those influences ordinarily accredited in Venus as of the beautiful, as of the music, as of those factors in same, as that which may bridge often that which is lacking in this full trust.

The influences of Saturn make for the changes that have been at definite periods in the experience of the entity in the present sojourn, and into the way of its mental thinking—not only that but as to the environmental forces or influences, and the manner of application as related to same.

Mars has made for those forces where anger, wrath and the like have become such at times that the necessity of choice became paramount to be weighed with those innate feelings that all of such experiences are worthy of being considered, and not thrown aside lightly; neither are they to be dwelt upon in such measures or manners as to become paramount.

For the creating of anger breeds contempt. Contempt gone to fruition breeds strife, and makes for disturbing forces that become—in the experiences of the entity—those things that bring inharmony.

Reading 1510-1   F 22

These records as we find are rather out of the ordinary. The interpretations of these should bring much into the experience of the entity in the present, if there is the application of those activities necessary for the entity to give expression to that which has been builded—not only in the experiences of the entity in the earthly sojourns but from the astrological aspects.

For this entity should become a real influence and power. Be sure this is used CONSTRUCTIVELY in the experience in this sojourn, for not only may fortune and fame be the entity's but the many will be influenced by the choices made by the entity in its activities in this experience.

In giving the interpretations then of that as we find has been the record of the entity's thought and purpose upon the skein of time and space, or upon God's book of remembrance—For as Time and Space are manifestations of Divinity in the experience of individuals in material plane, the other—Patience—must be ever an attribute of an entity in making application of self and self's virtues; overcoming faults or correcting this or that in the experience, for then ye may find these will work together for good in the experience.

Then, in giving the interpretations, we choose that as may be the more helpful of the experiences in the earth. For what ye are is the result of what ye have been, in applying in thy associations and relations to others the laws of divinity, of truth, of life everlasting.

The astrological aspects we find become rather the weakening influences than as the applications have been in the material sojourns. Yet all urges are only the direction in which the entity may take choice, and it is then by choice and by will as to what one does about those things that become as opportunities or experiences in the dealings and associations, and in the activities in this material plane.

In the astrological we find Venus as the RULING influence; also Jupiter, and Saturn—and Mars; these becoming influences by that which has been attributed to the various planets, because of the activities of the entity in those ENVIRONS; rather than because the entity was born when Venus or Jupiter or Mars or any of these were in the ascendency or descendency. Because these become a part of the influence by the application!

Knowledge is well, but knowledge without the works or without the application is worse than useless.

And being forewarned, be forearmed; and know that what thou choosest in every direction must in its SPIRITUAL import be of a CONSTRUCTIVE nature.

Then ye will find that indeed as ye sow, so will ye reap.

For today is set before thee life and death, good and evil; choose thou.

In Venus we find the inclinations towards that of the beautiful, the loving; the INTUITIVE influences, those of a sympathetic nature—yet seeing the beauty and the activities in individuals as well as things.

Yet there is the inclination to rely upon others for the help and aid, which becomes a weakening influence. For know, while self should never become wholly sufficient unto self, that ye may accomplish has been accomplished in thine own experience through thine own activities among thy fellow man!

Hence ye will find that relying upon the good that arises from the counsel to the Spirit within will direct, rather than the soft words of those though they may be pleasant in thine ears.

Not sacrifice always, no. Rather mercy and judgement, that there be kept in the experience the beauty that ye see in nature, in the activities, in the influences.

For there are the abilities to depict characterizations in the activities of natures to bring to their individual consciousnesses the good or bad, as may be chosen by those influences that are harbored in the minds of individuals.

For Mind IS the Builder, whether material or spiritual—as the mind is both material and spiritual-minded as it were. For it takes hold upon life and death.

Hence keep thy mind in those activities in which constructive influences and forces are ever the guiding light in thy choices.

In Jupiter we find the influence for the activity to be associated with masses, groups, crowds, nations; rather than a definite direction in individual activity.

While the influence may be exerted by self, and is exerted by self—but as has been indicated, the influence will be to the groups and to the masses; yea, even to nations, in their choice of words, in their choice of activities; yea, even in their choice of associations—by that ye may bring to their consciousness in thy dealings with them through thy art, thy activities, thy associations in the material things.

Keep the individuals, however, spiritual-minded; not as of rote but because it IS constructive and IS a growth or a growing thing. For ye grow in grace and knowledge and in the understanding as ye apply same in thy associations with others day by day.

In Mars we find anger; this making for rather the associations ABOUT the entity. For the natural placidness, even temperament from Venus as we find makes for rather these influences from without.

Then be not too quick in thy judgements of others. Put thyself in their place, in thy mind, before ye pass judgements on others.

The influences from the activities in that ever-changing force (Saturn) are indicated in the experience, in that there will be many changes and environs of the entity under many circumstances and activities.

Yet these may be experienced by thy holding to the love—not of self but rather of the help, the hope that ye may bring to others in thy way of choice of activities in thy dealings with them in every form and manner.

Reading 1620-2   F 44

In giving the interpretations of the records as we find them, these are chosen with the desire to make the experience a helpful one in the present activities of the entity.

While the faults as well as the virtues are drawn, these are given that the entity—or with the desire that the entity may see self; and thus, having set its ideal, enable self to turn more to the within.

The natural inclinations of the entity to drift here or there, or to be overenthusiastic about this or that movement or activity—today one and tomorrow another, oft leave the entity with the experience—in its enthusiasm—of having expended all the glow or gloss or foam, and being left with the dregs only.

Oft such activity tends to make for questionings on the part of others. This also causes confusions and doubts. For the entity finds individuals or groups enthusiastic today, and tomorrow entirely lost in the activity of such as may for the moment be a very promising experience for the entity.

It is well, then, that the entity take all of those inclinations as may be presented and analyze them within the experience of self; and know that what is everyone's business is nobody's business. While, to be sure, it is well to analyze and to have advice or counsel from this or that student of this or that thought or activity, the real analysis must come from within. For it is with what measure ye mete that it is measured to thee again.

Then it is well that there be the answer from within. For until the individual becomes enthusiastic over any movement or any activity in which it may engage itself so as to be CONSISTENT in same, it has not begun to take hold.

So it is well that self know self and what is the ideal; not only in what ye believe but as to Who is the author of what ye believe. Be sure that the author is able to supply mentally, physically—and above all, spiritually—that as may be the answer for every experience; whether it be in turmoil or in peace, in harmony or in discord.

For that which answers not ALL is to the inner self only half a truth.

In giving the astrological aspects, and the urges that arise in the experience of the entity from same, know that these are only innate—or are activated upon by choices that are made by the entity in relationships to same.

For as the body is made up in the present of the physical, the mental and the spiritual aspects, so each in its turn has its influence according to the choice the entity makes.

Then the end thereof, which is free-will, may be known and given a helpful force in whatever direction it is chosen.

Rather than these astrological aspects being an influence because the Sun, the Moon or the Planets may be under certain zodiacal signs when the entity enters, we find that they are in such positions because of what the entity has done! and these then are influences because of the associations of the real or soul self in that environ, rather than because of their material aspect or influence upon the activity of the entity.

For as the entity is a part of the whole, as the entity may attune itself to the universal consciousness as may manifest within, thus it is a part of the whole and not ruled by any portion of same—save as the will allows same to become the motivative force for any given activity.

The Moon was a sojourn [in consciousness] of the entity. Hence oft in the developing years, though beautiful in body and in manner of expression, in its association, the entity was always called fickle—or changeable. This is a part of the entity's experience, and yet—as the entity would express self—it never intended to be such. But there are the emotions and the activities. Hence there are the needs for the entity to make for the finding of the self and the purpose and the desire within.

Jupiter is a benevolent influence or association, or desire for the entity to impress or to be activative or dependent upon or to influence great masses of people. But know it must be individual. Do not seek to make others that you would not be yourself. Ye may not climb up higher than thine own ideal. Ask not others to do that ye would not do yourself.

Also we find Venus in its beautiful aspects as an influence in the experiences of the entity. Hence easily does the entity influence or control individuals, but just as easily does the entity find that—as the entity would give expression—so few are dependable! Why?

Ask that within self and know the answer is within self, as much as or more than within the others. For thou art a part of the whole.

The Uranian influences also make for the sudden changes, as well as interests in the occult or mysterious forces; and the natures of things as in their extremes are a part of the entity's experiences.

As we find, such astrological influences or urges arise through the innate mental forces; while the emotions arise from the sojourns of the entity in the material plane.

These as we find (the material sojourns) have been very, very far apart; not a great many in number, yet not all of these are given, for not all influence the entity in the experiences of the present activity—but arise from the emotional forces, or through the emotional forces of the body.

Reading 2397-1   F 42

In giving the interpretations of the experiences of the entity—these are so varied that they might be termed at first, even to the entity, as being fantastic. Yet, remember—and in the analyzing of self and of self's problems—the lesson that is to be learned here and now. And know that thou art NEVER alone if ye hold to that purpose that ye may be at one with Him. For His promise has been, "I will not leave thee—I will be with thee always." And again may ye, in seeking—oft—oft—hear that voice within, "Be not afraid, it is I."

We find that the astrological aspects have their influence. For the entity, the soul, being oft in that environ of material consciousnesses, is of a high temperament; with deep convictions, deep earnestness towards spiritual aspects, and NOT in that direction of material temperaments as many an entity might be who is termed "sensitive."

For, the entity is sensitive—but in quite a different way from that of the purely materialistic intent.

Hence the dreams, the visions, the desires and hopes, are far ahead of that which, apparently, the entity is able to manifest, or to materialize.

The entity then at times grows weary with the struggle; at times feels almost like quitting the chase, the seeking.

PATIENCE! For in same ye become—as the Way hath given—aware of thy relationships to the Father-God.

Astrologically, then, we find that Venus, Mercury, Uranus and Neptune become rather the ruling forces.

Jupiter's influence is just that seeking—as yet—to be made more manifest in the dealings with and relationships to others.

In Venus we find abilities for manifesting love, art, nature; those things that make for expressions of affection, of hope, of those influences that are indeed the seed of the spirit. Lose not thy hold on same!

We find in Mercury rather the practicality of the entity, and this at times may become the stumbling block, even to the entity. For this, as combined with those experiences in materiality, has brought hardships of a material nature; yet satisfactions and longings—as will be indicated—for the seeking of expression as may accomplish that so sought.

In Uranus we find the extremes, and yet the abilities oft to make the voices of colors, of harmonies, applicable in the experiences of that being attempted or done.

Know that only in Him, the Way, do such extremes meet. For, remember, as may be manifested in self, in materiality, He came unto His own, and His own received Him not. There was not anything made that was made, save through Him. His consciousness then was in materiality, with the abilities to manifest in the lives and the experiences of others not only the mysteries of ages but of the future; and yet it is He that may be, that will be, thy hope, they companion in thy endeavors—if ye but entertain Him in thine own heart, purpose and desires!

In Neptune we find the mystical influences become a deeper portion of the inner consciousness of the entity. Thus we find an unusual manifestation in this entity of much that is incomprehensible to some, and yet capable of being made manifest in the experiences of the many—if the entity will but hold to that which is needed in the experience.

5

●

Sample Edgar Cayce Life Readings

Reading 294-19 M 47 (Edgar Cayce Life reading on himself)—entire reading

This Psychic Reading given by Edgar Cayce in two sessions at his office, 322 Grafton Avenue, Dayton, Ohio, this 28th day of February, 1925, and March 6,1925 [both at 5:10 P.M.] in accordance with request made by self, Mr. [294].

PRESENT

Edgar Cayce; Linden Shroyer, Conductor; Gladys Davis, Steno. Mrs. Edgar Cayce and Hugh Lynn Cayce.

READING

Born March 18, 1877, in Christian Country, near Hopkinsville, Kentucky. Time of Reading 322 Grafton Ave., 5:10 P. M. Dayton Time. Dayton, Ohio.

LS: You will give the relation of this entity and the Universe, and the Universal Forces, giving the conditions that are as personalities latent and exhibited in the present life. Also the former appearances in the earth's plane, giving time, place, name, and that in that life which built or retarded the development for the entity, giving the abilities of the present entity and to that which it may attain, and how.

EC: Yes, we have the entity here and that relation that has to do with the Universal Forces as are shown in the earth's plane, and the connections with the present sojourn in the earth's plane.

As we see, we have had many of these conditions in part before. Here we may find them in a more complete outline.

In the sojourn in the present earth's plane, we find the entity took its position from that of Uranus, with the elements of Venus, Neptune, Jupiter and Mercury, with the affliction in Mars and Saturn. In this sojourn in the relations with other planets, we find the entity having passed through all the stages, or planes, yet returning in the earth's plane for that merited in the earth plane return through Saturn's forces for the again development in the Universal Forces as are applied to the manifestations of soul and spirit entities through the physical or earth plane.

Then, as we see in the present earth plane, while the entity has reached that plane where the mental and the environmental forces in present plane have set many of the conditions for the present sojourn, yet there are many urges to be satisfied, reached, known, accomplished, found, yet, in the earth's plane. Many may be reached. Others may be lost.

Then we have with reference to the sojourn in the other spheres, and in this plane, these urges in the individuality of the entity:

One to many peoples very contradictory in thought, action and deed. One little understood or comprehended by the greater mass of people. One who may reach those developments were the urge kept in the manner where the understanding could be given to other individuals. Lacking in this, as we shall see the cause.

In the mental urges we find that of the universality in the Jupiter forces, yet ever with the Venus forces dominant in entity's action, and with these often with Mars' influence brings condemnation to the entity.

One given to be very eccentric in many ways. One that finds very little of the level, or the capacity to be moderate in any, either very much in one condition or another. One spending much of the energies to whatever undertaken. This again we find often brings the destructive elements, or the misunderstandable efforts to much that might be accomplished in a more moderate manner.

One that will have the more cares in the later days as pertaining to the understandable things in Universal Forces. One that may give much to the Universe through the touch as is made in that of the Uranian and of the forces as are in Neptune, yet one not having reached the highest development that may be attained in these spheres. For the entity should be near large bodies of water, that the urge may be reached through that element that is given from the bigness of such bodies, that are elemental in their manner of bringing urge to other individuals that may be awakened, through the elements of mental, spiritual and mystic forces.

One we find that has many conditions to meet, brought more particularly by the misunderstanding of self and the inability of the entity to control self in any moderate way. One that brings much element of the forces in wrath that gives misunderstanding to others. This all we see reached through lack of control of will and self as has been set for the entity in the present earth's plane, for as has been given, the entity of an individual entering the earth's plane, while the urge is set from the individual's sojourn in other spheres, the environment of the individual, and the will of the entity, either build or mar the development through that individual sojourn in earth's plane, for in the flesh we find the mental, soul and spirit becomes the subjugation to the wishes, the desires, of the carnal forces, and in other spheres those of the elements pertaining to that sphere and the urge then of the individual in earth's plane is governed by the direction in which these are guided—urges. In this entity then we find there are many in the present sphere not guided in the manner that the development has been to that point where it should be.

In the appearances, then, as we shall see, there has come much of those elemental forces entering in, both from the sphere and from earthly sojourn in the earth. In the appearances, then:

Before this we find that the entity was in that of the wanderer that came to the present land in John Bainbridge, and the entity then rather that of one lost to those directions as were given under the tutelage and the directions of those in whose care the entity was committed, [in the French incarnation just preceding it] and with the change in the environment in that earth plane then brought, the entity lost itself and its development in the earth's plane. For it became a wanderer in the land. While contacting many peoples, yet many peoples suffered in the wake of the individual. Hence the early return to the earth's plane and the wanderings to and fro through many of the scenes that the entity experienced at that time. The entity then we see was in the earth's plane in 1742.

In the one before this we find the entity then in the French Court and in the days of Louis the 15th, and in the household of the monarch, though separated then from the care of those who lacked the influence in the life in the earth's plane of receiving the forces in the surrounding conditions to bring development in the earth's plane, being then only in that of the small child, or living only to the age of five. In this personality as exhibited through this condition, we find more given in the one following this in that of Bainbridge than in the present earth's plane. Still there is in the innate forces that desire to seek out the individuals who have the greatest attention put to those that lose the influences of the mother and those forces surrounding same.

In the one before this we find in that of the Grecian forces, when the gates were stormed in the Trojan Wars, and the entity then a defender at that gate, losing the life, and the development in that plane came through the hardships as were experienced by the physical body. There being many then in the earth's plane with which the body will be and is associated in the present earth's plane. For the cycle of life's forces and of earth's influence in relative forces, manifested in the Universe, brings many of that period in the present earth's period. The personalities that are exhibited in the present plane are those of the inability to control self in manner when there are those conditions that bring wrath or displeasure to the entity, making one then that has the quick temper in most unexpected circumstances and conditions. This, as we see, then, was not a plane of development in earth's sphere and these urges from that are yet to be overcome in the present earth's plane.

In the one before this we find in that of plainsman, as has been given, and those conditions that surrounded the entity then at that time make for the entity the greatest force in the present earth's plane, and the seeking out of that entity through which the greatest development in that sphere came, the entity brings the greater development in the present plane, as well as often the greatest worries and troubles. For, being unable to correlate those conditions, we find these make many combative conditions in that sphere and from those conditions. For from this plane we find the greater forces as are manifest through the psychic forces, occult forces, mind development, come from experiences in that sojourn, correlated with the spiritual development in the Uranian forces which become accentuated at the present time through the entity.

As to the personalities exhibited in the entity in the present, we find that ability to apply, when the conscious forces are laid aside, the development reached in that sphere, and the forces of the universal forces become a part. Hence the abilities of the entity in all psychic force, which is the extenuation, as it were, of that plane, and is either modified for the good or for the bad, by, through, or in the manner in which the suggestion for such development, such manifestation, such desire of knowledge, is approached; and the greater coming, as has been given, through that of the mind that holds self in that of the receptive mode, or the negative forces. For the entity through its experiences becomes the great dynamic force in positive action. Hence the relations as are given, reaching many spheres of universal knowledge and force, whether of animal, vegetable, mineral, or of the universal knowledge in that of mental, soul or spiritual development. And the entity's sojourn, and the conditions brought in the physical plane, we find giving then the greater urge for the physical conditions in bodies, when guided in that channel; yet through the urge as received may, with the other forces, give of all the forces as may be brought to the force of the given conditions as are reached through suggestion to mental conditions.

In the one before this we find the entity was in the Egyptian land, when the force of the law was being given to the people, in that one chosen as the highest authority in the mental attributes, acting in the way of the Priest [Ra-Ta] to the people, being the first chosen priest of the cult, as afterward called, among the nations of the world. In the present personality and present plane, we find again many in the earth's plane and associated with the entity, that were associated with the entity in that plane. Again we find the entity falling in the way of flesh, for the entity represented that as has been given in the written word, "The Sons of God looked upon the daughters of men and saw they were fair and good to look upon," [Gen. 6:2] and through this fleshly carnal force brought destructive elements to the entity. In the present plane we find still that same urge to be overcome in the entity, for there is that innate call and desire in the flesh for those fleshpots again, as called, of Egypt, and the entity needs that to keep the forces of mental and spiritual development ever to press onward to the higher forces.

In the one before this we find in the first, when the forces in flesh came to dwell in the earth's plane. The entity was among the first to inhabit the earth in that form, and was from that of the beginning in earth's plane, when referred to as the human form dwelling in the earth's forces. In this we find the larger development in the entity, for then [the soul was] able to contain in the Oneness of the forces as given in the Sons of Men, and realizing the Fatherhood of the Creator.

In the present plane we find that ever urge to be drawn nearer to the spiritual elements of every force. Hence in the summing up and use of these, let the entity keep the spiritual forces ever magnified, in action, deed and in truth. For, in earth's plane, every element of the physical or mental, or spiritual nature, is judged by the relation to spiritual forces.

As to the abilities of the entity, we find the entity capable of making the success in any line of endeavor, especially along those of healing arts, or of the higher arts as are contained in the spiritual development through the earth's plane.

Then use those forces as are in hand and magnify His name through the world, for in so doing the entity will save self and others. For as destructive forces have entered in through the entity's physical sojourns, so must the rebuilding, resuscitating, re-establishing, reincarnated forces of the entity be manifest in the present.

We are through for the present.

Reading 257-201   M 45   (Life reading for sales manager)—entire reading

This Psychic Reading given by Edgar Cayce at his home on Arctic Crescent, Virginia Beach, Va., this 4th day of September, 1938, in accordance with request made by self——Mr. [257], Active Member of the Ass"n for Research & Enlightenment, Inc.

PRESENT

Edgar Cayce; Gertrude Cayce, Conductor; Gladys Davis, Steno. Mr. [257].

READING

Born April 22, 1893, in Lexington, Ky. Time of Reading 4:25 to 5:10 P.
M. Eastern Standard Time. New York City.

GC: You will give the relation of this entity and the universe, and the
universal forces; giving the conditions that are as personalities, latent
and exhibited, in the present life; also the former appearances in the
earth's plane, giving time, place and the name, and that in each life
which developed or retarded the development of the entity; giving the
abilities of the present entity, and that to which it may attain and how.
You will also give him an outline for the developing of his service to his
family, associates, and mankind for the balance of the days of his life,
to improve mentally, physically, spiritually; with warnings of things to
avoid and plans and advice for accomplishment.

EC: Yes, we have the records here of this entity—these we have had
before; the astrological sojourns or urges from the environs about the
earth and those from the material sojourns in the earth.

In giving then that as we find which would be the more helpful
and beneficial to the entity in the application of self in the present
experience, we would analyze for the moment the appearances in the
earth—and that manner in which the entity applied self or failed in the
experience; giving then that first which is the purpose for the entering
of a soul, an entity, into material experience.

Naturally, in the mind of the entity, with its studies, with its application of the experiences through which it has passed and is passing, and
is to experience as well as those conditions that are of a local, a national,
an international consequence—not only as related to the entity as an
individual of a country, of a faith, but of a peoples—all of these must
be taken into consideration.

But first let's begin with that premise from which there is a reasoning.
And, as is well or better understood by the entity, owing to its material
experiences through the sojourns in the earth of such a varied nature,
all must answer to a something within—before it may be made a part
of the entity and the entity's experiences.

Each soul as it has entered and does enter into material manifestation is to fulfill a purpose, with the Creative Forces or God. For He hath
not willed that any soul should perish, but hath with every temptation,

every fault, prepared a way, a manner, an opportunity for the entity to become as one with Him.

For that is the purpose of the soul's being in the beginning. Hence without beginning, without end.

Hence as we find, when souls sought or found manifestation in materiality by the projection of themselves into matter—as became thought forms—and when this had so enticed the companions or souls of the Creator, first we had then the creation in which "God breathed into man (God-made) the breath of life and he became a living soul," with the abilities to become godlike.

Hence we find the first preparation or estate, or manner in which those souls might through material manifestation acclaim—by the living, by the being—that which was and is and ever will be consistent with the purposes of creation—was given into the estate of man. [Atlantis?]

The entity was among those first who through those channels came into consciousness, awareness of the relationships of the material man to the Creative Forces; that came into material activity during the early portions of man's CONSCIOUSNESS of being an independent entity, or body, in a material existence. [Atlantis?]

Thence we find the entity passing through those experiences, becoming rather aware, with the sons of those activities in the experiences when all thought forms in matter were put away—through the experience of Noah. [2nd destruction of Atlantis portion by flood?]

Then we find the experience as the priest the entity became among the first to minister in the tabernacle in the wilderness. And there we find the entity as it were was persuaded into the offering of strange fires upon the alters. There we find the experiences that must be gained by the entity in its application of itself, its tenets in the present; as to the holiness of His commands and to know that they are as they were of old, "If ye will be my people, I will be thy God," and "Though ye wander to the far corners of the earth, if ye will call I will hear—and will answer speedily."

This is the call that the entity will arouse in the minds in the hearts of its fellow men in the present day; not by might nor by power as of man's edict but by the laws of the promises in Him—which in love may overcome. For He called to thee, He in that experience gave that into thy keeping which was holy; that ye alone of those of the priesthood might enter into the holy of holies. The strange fire then is rather that ye overstepped thy bonds and bounds in entering before thy day was called.

But know that today, EVERYWHERE, He has called that if ye will but put thy trust alone in Him, He will lift thee up. Thy enemies, thy persecutors, thy activities shall become not as a people, not as a man, but as God hath wrought. For though the heavens and the earth pass away, His promises to thee—AS the son of Aaron—will NOT pass from thee, UNTIL AGAIN—as ye did in Shiloh—ye shall KNOW the truth and the truth shall make thy people free! [Ex. 24?]

Hence the activity that the entity is called to do in the present; not as a priest that is called apart, but rather as He gave in those days, "the time and times and a half times shall pass, and THEN shall man come to know that in the temple, in the tabernacle of his OWN temple will he meet his God face to face!"

That experience was countenanced, as it were, or a portion of the experience of the entity just before that—when in the Egyptian land the entity was as the aide to the Priest—yea, the defender even in the exile. It was tempered again in the position as a priest himself. [Ra-Ta Period]

Hence we find, from the paralleling, from the drawing from the experiences of the entity through those sojourns, there is a work, there is a service to be done to the fellow man. Not as proclaiming aloud from some housetop, but rather as ye sit in the quiet of thy home, as ye meet them in the daily walks of life, as ye counsel with them in thy daily activities; whether it be in the material relationships one to another or as counseling as a brother one to another.

These ALL become a part of the experience.

Arouse, ye people then of Levi! Harken to the voice of thy fathers! Hate not those precepts that have brought to thee the awareness of the needs of thy turning to the ways of thy God, but rather let the Lord thy God have His way with thee.

Again we see a portion of the activities of the entity, the soul, as it sought expression again in the rebuilding, the rehabitation of a destroyed purpose, a destroyed ideal; when there had come, as by word of mouth, that there was needs be that again there would be established, there must be established in Jerusalem a house, yea, the rebuilding of the walls and the reestablishing. There we find the entity was as the scribe to the teacher, the leader [Ezekiel] during those experiences. Hence we find that the priest of the day, yea the warrior Nehemiah, yea the priest or scribe Ezre, all were a part of the activities of the entity.

Hence through the experiences of the entity in the present sojourn we have found that not only in its own land but in others it has been called into service to act in the capacity of one to bring even material as well as mental and spiritual messages to his peoples.

These become again then a part of the entity's activities in the present sojourn. For it is to put as it were the words into the mouth of those that are downcast, to those that are gone astray; in bringing condemnation to those in authority of MAN'S making but rather turning them to the Lord, to serve Him, to raise again that stone, that Eben-ezer [1 Sam. 7:12] within the own conscience, the own heart, as to thy promise to thy God and His promises to thy people; that if ye will turn again and serve Him, and putting away those slick practices, those strange conditions, ye shall SUCCEED in thy material undertakings! For the Lord being on thy side, who can be against thee!

This is the message ye must put into the hearts and minds of those who have become afraid because of the edicts of those in power. But there is no power given except it is lent of the Lord! Those He loveth He chasteneth and purgeth every one. But if ye will but turn—lift up thy heart, thy face to His purposes, His ways—He will bring a great light unto the peoples of promise. For thou art among those that have, even in thy faulty ways, shown the way to the understanding; and in thus doing ye may walk again in the pathways that are straight, in those ways and understandings that will bring to thy experiences the knowledge that God IS in His holy temple, let all the earth keep silent —and He will bring it to pass! For it is His promise unto the sons of thy fathers and unto thee!

When the experiences of the entity were in the activities of the temple and the replenishing [rebuilding of the walls], we find much of the materials of the reestablishing of the old days. It is then any wonder that to even thy friends and thy neighbors it is given in thy daily labors that ye encourage them to those of period furnishings, period furniture, or to those things that will bring again to remembrance what their fathers thought and did, what their purposes were?

For as ye have chosen and have come into a land that is the home of the free, the home of the brave, where man may worship according to the dictates of his own conscience, and every man stands before God as an entity, recognizing that each is His child and is to fulfillthose purposes for which there was GIVEN the opportunity of a body that it might be used unto the glory of the Creator, then know:

The body is as nothing but a casement for the mind, the soul—that is precious in His sight. He hath not willed that any soul should perish, but has again and again called to the children, to His children, "If ye will but harken I will bless thee, that my name shall be precious among the children of men—as among those that are called to be as the lights and channels through which the preservation of my name shall be established."

As we find from the entity's activities through the sojourn as the soldier, there are the attempts to keep a unison among those of brethren. This in the face of present experiences may appear to have been a bad choice, yet filling those purposes, those commands of its superior officers in a way and manner as to bring commendation; not only to the peoples who were the physical foes but to those of its OWN company—as one that would bring help and aid to brethren. [Aide to Gen. Howe]

Again we find in the material things the desire to be the soldier, the activities in such for a cause or for a purpose; keep as it were in the van [vein?] of not only ideals but purposes through the experiences. [World War I]

These having passed, now arises the duties of the home, the duties among its associates, among its companions in this or that service or activity among his brethren.

What will ye make the harvest? What seed will ye sow?

Will ye put word by word, line upon line, precept upon precept, here a little, there a little, a reminder to all that they alone who love the Lord and His ways and His precepts SHALL succeed? whether they be in the position of affluence, in authority, or as the servant? They alone shall succeed, now or hereafter!

For the way ye know, and the truth ye have seen. The truth needs NO verification, but thy glorification in thy life, thy heart, thy manner of dealing with thy fellow man.

Ready for questions.

(Q) What can I do in reference to the Nazi situation in Germany and in America to again help the forlorn people? [World War II background]

(A) As has been indicated, by word, by manner of speech, by manner of living; that they turn again and raise that Eben-ezer, that promise made so long ago in the experiences of many, and yet is today, now, being met in the experiences of many. For each and every day the individual only meets himself. Then it is not by might, not by hate but by love of God; and the cry unto Him, and to turn to LOOK to Him FOR aid, for succor! For the hills and the valleys, the cattle and the gold are His; and if ye will turn to Him thy voice will be heard.

We are through for the present.

Reading 3902-2   M 40
Life reading for fireman)—entire reading

This Psychic Reading given by Edgar Cayce at the office of the Association, Arctic Crescent, Virginia Beach, Va., this 25th day of March, 1944, in accordance with request made by the self——through wife——Mrs. [2602], Associate Member of the Ass"n for Research & Enlightenment, Inc.

PRESENT

Edgar Cayce; Gertrude Cayce, Conductor; Gladys Davis, Steno. (Notes read to and transcribed by Jeanette Fitch.) Harmon Bro.

READING

Born October 8, 1903, in New London, Connecticut. Time of Reading 3:55 to 4:25 P. M. Eastern War Time. ..., Conn.

GC: You will give the relations of this entity and the universe, and the universal forces; giving the conditions which are as personalities, latent and exhibited in the present life; also the former appearances in the earth plane, giving time, place and the name, and that in each life which built or retarded the development for the entity; giving the abilities of the present entity, that to which it may attain, and how. You will answer the questions, as I ask them:

EC: Yes, we have the records here of that entity now known as or called [3902].

In giving the interpretations of the records, written or imposed or impressed upon the skein of time and space, or the Akashic records in

God's book of remembrances, these we find:

We would choose from these records that which if applied in the experience will bring a better interpretation of the how and why that there are certain latent and manifested urges in the abilities of the entity in the present, which if applied in a constructive, creative way may bring a better ability of the entity to apply itself in being a channel, a manifestation of those divine influences that are the cause and purpose of the entity's appearance in the earth in the present.

That an individual entity is aware of a physical, mental, soul longing in this material consciousness should in itself be evidence to the individual entity that the first cause, the God principle, the divine consciousness is aware of the entity and has been and is giving an opportunity to the entity for expression in this particular period of experience.

For He, thy God, hath need of thee. Thou hast need of Him if ye would be a channel of manifestation of the gift of consciousness at this particular period.

We would minimize the faults, we would magnify the virtues. For this is grace, this is mercy that is meted to thee. though ye find at times in thine own consciousness that ye feel far off, know that it is in Him that ye live and move and have thy being, and that His promise has been, "If ye call I will hear and answer speedily."

The conditions, then, are ever conditional. There is much for thee to do. For He hath given thee body, mind and soul. These are as manifestations of thy consciousness of Father, Son and Holy Spirit. Thy body is indeed the temple of the living God. Then in thy dealings with thine own body, thine own mind, thine own soul, act as though it were a consciousness. As ye act and as ye speak, and as ye apply, ye will become more and more aware. For as He has given, in patience, in perseverance, ye become aware of thy soul. Are ye in attune, then, with that consciousness? It is up to thee.

The spirit is willing. Will ye strengthen thy soul purpose? Will ye attune thy mind? Will ye act in thy body in such measures and manners that ye may know? For He hath promised, "If ye open the door, I will enter and abide with thee—I will walk with thee." It is up to thee.

As urges latent and manifested, many are the manifestations in the consciousness and in the urges of the entity indicating unusual abilities to manifest in a material world. From the urges, from sojourns during the interims we find Mercury, Mars, Venus, Jupiter. No better array might be set, and yet—as in spirit, so in mind—these must be attuned, used, applied. For though there may be purpose, ability, strength, without being used it is nil and of none effect.

In Mercury is the high mental ability.

We find in Mars the anxiety, wrath, madness, the abilities to do things; but they must be controlled by judgment, by the exercising of an ideal. Ye have a pattern that is set in Him and as given, "As ye would that men would do to you, do ye even so to them." This applied in every phase indicates an active principle and not merely a tenet to be set on Sabbath days or new moons or at some special occasion when you feel kindly towards one for a lovely deed done.

Love thine enemies also. Do good to them that hate you, and this will change and bring the exercising of patience that makes thee aware of thy oneness of purpose with that spirit which may guide you.

In Venus we find the consciousness of harmony, the ability to make good out of the voice—a speaking voice; a keen insight, the abilities to discern, and those little things that make up the consciousness, the awareness of good and evil. For it is line upon line, precept upon precept, here a little, there a little, not some great deed to be done, some great thing to be performed, but ye grow in grace, in knowledge, in understanding. Ye grow in making thyself a good husband, a good father, a good citizen. Not that ye become one suddenly because you've reached a certain age, position or place, because of thy financial or social position. But they are the way, even as He, thy ideal, thy Master is the way, the truth and the light, the word. These ye attain by practice.

We find in Jupiter the universal consciousness, the awareness as to the usage of things. Hence the entity's ability pertaining to watchfulness, and especially in Mars and Mercury things having to do with the mechanical or electrical.

As we could give, as we shall see from the application of the entity in and through earthly sojourns, the entity should begin now to study electronics. For as the earth and the peoples of same enter Aquarius, the air, we find that the electrical forces, electronics and energies are to be the ruling influences—by the very position of same in the spheres of the system which the earth occupies merely as a space or place in the present.

Hence the entity in those awarenesses and consciousnesses should prepare itself. And as ye feed the body that it may supply physical energies, so ye feed the mind and the soul that it, too, may attune and coordinate in building that which thyself, as an entity and as a child of the King may be filling that place He hath given thee to fill. For as ye take the first step, He prepares the way and He will not withhold any good thing from those who love His coming.

As there is not the time or ability to set aside certain periods for such training, do take a correspondence course in electronics. And as thy body rests, as thy body takes on understanding and knowledge, it may apply itself in a correspondence course in such a way that, as the changes are wrought by the periods of reconstruction, ye will find thy place in same and ye will grow with thy mind and thy soul, physically.

As to the appearances in the earth, we find that these have been quite varied. Not all may be given by any means but these that are a part of the awareness or consciousness of the entity in the present cycle of its experience. And these are at that period that they may be applied. As indicated the mental is to be applied for the development of the material as well as the mental and spiritual self. Keep self from condemnation ever.

Before that the entity was in the land of the present nativity when there were those changes being wrought by the rediscovering of principles as applied to light and heat.

Then in the name Don Collett (?) about New Haven and Cambridge, the entity applied self in using such for the construction. So may the entity in self in the present use those various elements, as changes are being wrought, for not only heat and light but as the answer to color, tone, voice, and the transportation of every sort or nature.

Before that the entity saw those activities in which there was either the compliance with or defiance of natural laws, in the period when the Master walked in the earth.

These are still the mysteries to the entity. But natural laws are God's laws. Everything in the earth is ruled by law. He said "Let there be light," and there was light—by law.

What law? Of the spirit of truth, of light itself moving into activity; thus becoming creative by law.

Learn ye then the spiritual law which ye attempted to understand, which ye studied then in the name Hedth.

The entity was an associate of Peter and John, eventually becoming a follower when the entity had been converted from the using of same as a material blessing.

For the universal blessing is, "As ye would that others should do to you, do you even so to them," not do others, lest they do thee; not to use brotherly love as something to build other than greater brotherly love or patience.

Before that the entity was in the Egyptian land when there were the preparations in the Temple of Sacrifice.

The entity was among those prepared for using electrical forces for light, heat, sound, transportation.

Thus as indicated, through these channels the entity may apply itself as it goes on in its present activity, for those changes that may be wrought in its experience.

But live the life for thy son, for thy neighbor, for thy brother, for thy friend, for thy foe. For this must be the consciousness in thee, that this is God's earth, God's world, God's consciousness that must be made manifest among men.

Begin in thine own self and with the one next to thee, and that which is not applicable in the life of thy son, of thy wife, of thy brother, ye cannot apply in a universal sense. Begin with self. Find the peace in self and ye will find that ye can bring it to others. For as indicated, "It must needs be that offenses come," that disturbances arise, but fear not, for thy Ideal has overcome the world. And as ye abide only in Him may ye be at peace with the world.

Ready for questions.

(Q) *What are the indications of future promotion in my present work?*

(A) Very good if there is the application of the spiritual truths in the material associations.

(Q) *Is there some other line of work I would be better fitted for?*

(A) Read what has been indicated, as to that ye may grow to, if ye seek to apply same in the present.

(Q) *Would it be advisable to ask for a transfer from my present assignment now?*

(A) We would not. We would work where we are and prepare self for other advancements that will come with same.

(Q) Is there any indication that a paid department will be established here in the near future?

(A) This should have little to do with thee. There will be a new department established but use it to help others, and use self in the manner indicated to advance further still.

We are through for the present.

Reading 2620-2   F 41   (Life reading for housewife and mother)—entire reading

This Psychic Reading given by Edgar Cayce at the home of Mrs. Robert R. M. Emmet, 1 Grace Church St., Rye, New York, this 24th day of November, 1941, in accordance with request made by the self—Mrs. [2620], Associate Member of the Ass"n for Research & Enlightenment, Inc., Virginia Beach, Va.

PRESENT

Edgar Cayce; Gertrude Cayce, Conductor; Gladys Davis, Steno. Mrs. [2620].

READING

Born April 20, 1900, in Budapest, Hungary. Time of Reading 10:50 to 11:40 A. M. Eastern Standard Time. ..., New York.

GC: You will give the relation of this entity and the universe, and the universal forces; giving the conditions which are as personalities, latent and exhibited in the present life; also the former appearances in the earth plane, giving time, place and the name, and that in each life which built or retarded the development for the entity; giving the abilities of the present entity, that to which it may attain, and how. You will answer the questions, as I ask them:

EC: (In going back over years from the present—"—'34—changes—'29—anxieties—'21—change—'12—changes again—" etc., on back to birth date.)

Yes, we have the record here of that entity now known as or called [2620].

In giving the interpretations of the records as we find them, much should be interpreted in the experiences of the entity in this present sojourn; that there may be the better application of the abilities that have been attained by the entity in its application of truth, love, life, understanding, in this present experience.

These interpretations we choose, then, with the desire and purpose that this may be a helpful experience for the entity; enabling the entity to better fulfill those purposes for which it entered this present sojourn.

It is true for the entity, and for most individual souls manifesting in the earth, that nothing, no meeting comes by chance. These are a design or pattern. These patterns, however, are laid out by the individual entity. For, there are laws. For law is love, love is law. And He hath not willed that any soul should perish, but hath with each temptation, each trial, prepared a way of escape.

Thus as the pattern of life, of consciousness, when the individual entity is to make application of that the entity has interpreted in its experience as related to the spiritual, the mental and the material laws, these then become active—the law of love—in the experience of the entity.

It is true, then, that there are latent and manifested urges, manifested abilities, manifested virtues, manifested faults, in the experience of each entity. These faults, these virtues may be pointed out, yet the usage, the application of same is of free will—that which is the universal gift to the souls of the children of men; that each entity may know itself to be itself and yet one with the universal cause.

Thus the pattern, the book of life is written by the entity in its use of truth, knowledge, wisdom, in its dealings with its fellow man through the material sojourns. Also during the interims between such sojourns there are consciousnesses, or awarenesses. For, the soul is eternal, it lives on, has a consciousness in the awarenesses of that which has been builded.

The awarenesses are a pattern of that we call astrological aspects. Not because the entity in a physical consciousness sojourned in any of the planets that are a part of this present solar experience, but each planet is accredited with certain environmental influences that are represented in the characteristics of each individual soul.

Thus, as we find in this entity, they give expression in the abilities, which find manifestation in the material body through developments or attunements in the glandular system of the body FOR material expression.

Thus upon the skein of time and space is the record of each soul made. In patience, in persistence may such be read.

Thus the interpretations chosen here are made with the desire that they be of a helpful influence to this entity.

In Venus we find the greater ruling influence; afflicted, as may be astrologically termed, in the Moon. Thus we find, in this entity, one beautiful in purpose, in hopes, in desires; of the universal nature. Oft not understood by those where that of material love life would find expression. For, these naturally attract opposites, and thus is growth ever made in a material expression. For, these are illustrated to the student, to those who would learn, in nature itself. Thus we find the love of mankind, the love of individual prospects. Those that are attracted to the entity are those who NEED the entity for that of, OFT, the sacrifice the entity must make in its own emotions to be of a helpful influence in the experience of the associate.

Thus may the world, may individuals find the entity as rather strange, rather distant; and yet the entity giving—giving of self makes ALL influences in the lives of those the entity meets BETTER for having known or been in association with the entity.

In Jupiter, both a benevolent and a questioned influence arises. Thus the universality of the entity's activities, of the entity's abilities, of the entity's virtues. These become influences in the mental forces, the mental abilities, yet—through these very Jupiterian and Venus influences—we find that the entity has attained the abilities to mentally and physically aid those who are in need of that to quiet the fears, to make RATIONAL that which arises from fear in the experience of others.

Thus the entity is given the ability as a healer, even through the laying on of hands, for those needing such as has been indicated.

We find in Uranus the extremes. Thus the changing influence that has been and is a part of the entity's experience. The associations bring such opposition, or such great opposites to that the entity itself attains or gains; thus bringing at times confusions, or wonderments, tears—and yet tears of joy at times. These are a part of the entity's experience in this sojourn.

Also there are the interests in the occult, the mystic, and—yea—abilities in creating, by the touch, those vibrations in the bodies to others as to become edifying in spirit, in mental abilities.

Thus these are the portions of the entity's experience that should be the greater stressed in the present.

As to the appearances or sojourns in the earth—these we find expressed or manifested in the material body through the senses. Do understand, do interpret the difference between the emotions that arise from the sensory system and those that arise from the GLANDULAR system alone. True, physically these interchange; yet one represents the WHOLE of the development, the other represents the step by step activity by an entity in its activity through the material world.

Not all of the sojourns are indicated as needed in the experience of the entity in the present for a helpful influence, but these are chosen that the entity may arouse more and more to those abilities that are a part of the experience of those virtues, as well as those faults. But in self, as in others, MAGNIFY the virtues, magnify the good, minimizing the faults. Not that good and bad do not exist. Each exists relatively in relationships to the awareness of the individual. Be aware of the good, see and hunt for, search out that which is good in each soul; thus magnifying that, the faults become less and less—this especially in associations in thine own household.

Before this the entity was in the land of the present sojourn, during the early periods of the settlings in the land now known as Rhode Island—or providence town, in those periods when Roger Williams made for those settlements there.

The entity was among the companions of the entity Williams, AS a companion then, in the name Martha Calvert.

In the experience the entity gained through its abilities to maintain friendly relationships not only with the natives of that land but the applying of herbs of the land, of the growths of the forest, to beneficial material gains for the peoples through that trying period.

Thus the love of nature, the love for peoples, the understanding of conditions. Tolerance the entity gained through that period.

The application of tolerance with patience, then, is needed in the present experience. For, as the entity aided then in bringing hope, through dispelling fear as to future activities, so there are the needs in the present for dispelling fear through faith, through the application of the latent and manifested abilities in its experience as it deals with its fellow men.

Know, ever, that law as indicated by Him, "Inasmuch as—or in the manner ye treat, ye respond to the least of thy fellow man, the same ye do unto thy Maker." Also as He gave, "In patience become ye aware of thy soul." These keep near to thy consciousness, in thy dealings with those about thee day by day.

Before that the entity was in the Holy Land, among the Roman peoples that were in high places during the sojourn of the Master in the earth.

And especially was the entity present (as has oft and may oft be a part of the present experience of the entity) during some of those periods when there were the trial, the Crucifixion. And the entity joined with the holy women in those periods when He was seen again, in that period of manifestation.

The name then was Amorela, and associated with those that kept guard at the temple. There the entity, at the trial before Pilate, in the throng, saw the face of the Master. The entity heard those words, saw that tenderness with which He felt and experienced His aloneness when deserted by those who had been close to Him. The entity was spoken to by the Master when He gave, "Be not afraid, for me nor for thyself. All is WELL with thee."

Thus, when there were those reports of His resurrection, when there were the attempts of the Romans to put aside the questionings of the Jews, the entity sought to know. And these periods brought disturbance to the entity, when it wept much. And this still finds expression in its attempt for vision.

KNOW, then, that the healing is ever in Him, and that to Him goes the credit of the abilities as manifest through thy hands, through thy voice, through thy pronouncements. To Him the love, the honor must ever be given.

In the experience the entity gained throughout. And do not fail in the present to keep that as was the pronouncement to thee, "Be not afraid. All is well with thee." For, as He hath given, "If ye love me ye will keep my commandments, and my commandments are not grievous,—only that ye love one another." These ye are manifesting. Keep them. Preserve them. Live them. Be them.

Before that the entity was in the Egyptian land, during those periods of reconstruction, when there was the choosing of individuals for the purification of activities, not only in the propagation but in the becoming of channels for those souls to manifest—as was taught through that period of activity.

The entity was purified in the Temple of Sacrifice, and became a channel that brought to the experience of many that which aided in the distribution of knowledge, of wisdom, as related to the material, the spiritual, the mental world of that period.

The name then was Ibd-Exr.

As to the abilities of the entity in the present, then, that to which it may attain, and how:

First, study to show thyself approved unto that ideal ye found and sought in Him, in the temple, or in the court at Pilate's condemnation period.

Hold to that as ye manifested in those experiences when ye saw Him bless those about Him, after the Resurrection.

Know then, in thine inner self, there is no other way.

Study to show thyself approved unto that ideal. Call upon Him often. Thus thy abilities to comfort, to encourage those who are weak, and mentally disturbed. And ye shall find rest in the consciousness of a life well used, and will enter into that peace, that joy as He alone can give.

Ready for questions.

(Q) What steps should I now take to make my life a greater service for humanity?

(A) Use thy abilities to heal, by the laying on of hands, by giving such suggestions that quiet the fears of those who are fearful and doubtful as to their relationships to the Creative Forces or God; thus bringing mental AND material health and joy to others.

(Q) Any advice regarding how to heal by laying on of hands?

(A) As has been given here, praying with others and letting the vibrations from self pass through or into their bodies. Not taking ON the vibrations, but laying them all on Him. For He IS the healer, He IS life. He overcame death, hell and the grave. He overcame temptation. And in Him is peace, harmony, life. With this accrediting, begin; not by proclaiming—for remember, as He oft gave, "Tell no man." Just be thyself, and thy trust in Him—and these bring the spirit of truth in thy labor of love for Him.

(Q) How have I been associated in the past with the following individuals, and how may I best help them in the present: First, my daughter, [...]?

(A) In the experience before this the daughter was a friend, that doubted the self then. In the Egyptian experience the daughter was THEN a daughter. Thus the relationships we find at present in which the daughter at periods doubts and resents, and yet periods when there is the turning to for counsel. Hence the usage or application—be patient, but instruct in that which is found expressed in the 14th and 17th of St. John.

(Q) *My husband, Kurt [...]?*

(A) In the Roman experience or activity we find that the associations were as companions then. There needs to be much patience. Not all of the pattern was straightened there. In the present keep the pattern in patience, in love. Let not thy heart be troubled; ye believe in God, believe also in Him who can keep thee ever in that peace—not as the world or material things give peace, but peace of spirit, of purpose, of heart.

Reading 259-8   F 18   (Life reading for young woman)—entire reading

This psychic reading given by Edgar Cayce at his home on Arctic Crescent, Virginia Beach, Va., this 4th day of September, 1934, in accordance with request made by the self——Miss [259], through Edgar Cayce himself——Honorary Member of the Ass"n for Research & Enlightenment, Inc.

PRESENT

Edgar Cayce; Gertrude Cayce, Conductor; Gladys Davis, Steno. Mildred Davis and L. B. Cayce.

READING

Born March 22, 1916, 11:45 P.M., in the old Union Street Hospital, cor. Union St. & McLeod Ave., Selma, Ala. Time of Reading 10:45 to 11:45 A. M. ..., Alabama. (Life Reading Suggestion)

EC: (Going back over the years towards birth date—"—33—32—31—30—Near accident in '30. 29—28," etc.)

Yes, we have the entity and those relationships with the universe and universal forces, that are latent and manifested in the personalities of the present entity, called [259].

In giving that which may be helpful to the entity in the present experience, some of those things, conditions or surroundings that might be helpful will be given, and then the why may be gathered from the experiences through which the entity in its earthly sojourns has passed.

The seal, or that which should be the motto of the body: A triad with the balance, Et Libra et Pura. These as a pin or an emblem or as a drawing would be well to have about the body at all times.

The colors, the odors, the body should keep about self: The odor, orris and lavender. The colors, white with not DEEP black but with shades; plain rather than brocaded or laces; that which is sometimes termed mannish, but rather the effeminate in the mannish style.

As to the astrological influences and the sojourns of the entity in those environs about the earth, only as mental influences may these be seen in the experience of the mental developments in the present sojourn. Being a body-physical in the present, through filial and material love the material things about the body will remain oft in strain until self has conquered self in its material desires and does not censure another nor find other than—in its daily experience—that which may be used as a stepping-stone for its soul, mental and material advancement. These come from sojourns in Jupiter, Uranus, Venus. Hence sentiment, the mental, the vision of power and activity in varied spheres of material expression will be the dreams of the body in its meditations in its inner self; and the expression that comes to the forefront must be tempered with mercy, justice and right, through the WILL of self. For, will is the factor that makes for growth in the soul's sleep through the earth's experience. For, with the birth of a physical body the soul slumbers; and its dreams are the deeds by which the soul is judged in its associations with its fellow man.

As to the appearances in the earth and those influences brought to bear upon the entity in its material, mental and spiritual developments in the present:

Before this we find in those environs of what is now known as Jamestown, Virginia, during the periods when there was the reestablishing or reenforcing of those that had come in these environs for the establishing of a material dwelling place in this land, the entity was among those that were born under that new regime when there had been the establishing of a government and the spreading out of those peoples into the adjoining vicinities.

Then the name was Bainbridge (Mary), the entity being of those that had come as the activities of one that had been a sojourner in this land; growing in the activities that went for the developments of those peoples to the bringing MORE of the people that were to aid in the further development for the land. The entity SOLD for the crown was claimed by same, through those in whose care the body–physical was given in the experience. Hence in associations with some of those that became the leaders in that particular vicinity, and associated the more closely with those that made for the establishing of that indicated in the seal—LIBERTY; for the entity was the associate of those that PROMPTED the activity of Henry; becoming a close active associate of those that made for the Custis, the Lees, the Randolphs, the Curtises, Lancasters, of this particular land.

Hence in the present the desires for those things pertaining to power in the fields of politics, and the entity COULD MAKE of itself and excellent politician—should it choose in these associations or environs to make its activities in that direction; yet, as we find, this is not the greater field for mental and soul development—as will be seen.

Before that we find the entity was in that land now known as the Roman, or rather the Grecian and Roman, during the periods when there were what are now known as the Trojan Wars, during the activities between those over that entity Helen of Troy.

During those activities the entity then was the companion of the assistant keeper of the gate to the city, and during the experience the drawings of the entity enabled those that were of the besieged to encounter—in part, in the main; though little credit was given Garcia in the experience, yet such enabled the armies—or the individual activities of those in Achilles' activities—to succeed in bringing destruction to Hector's forces. And the entity saw those activities.

Hence the abilities in the writing, or to depict by word or by drawing, or by the activities in the artistic temperament, arise from the associations in that experience.

The entity neither gained nor lost in the soul or inner development. In the material things, a success; yet these experiences will—through its developing years—play an important part, or impress or produce urges that may find expressions in the material activity of the entity. Yet, as is significant in the latter portion of the seal, purity of purpose, of mind, of body, must be kept if there would be the mental or the spiritual urge that will bring peace and harmony in the experience in this sojourn.

Before that we find the entity was in that land now known as the Arabian or Persian, during those sojourns or activities of the people that became the leaders in that land.

We find the entity then was the elder sister to that one who rose to be leader, or Uhjltd; for with the divisions of the people, with the turmoils that arose through the raids of Uhjltd's own people, the entity—then in the name Ujilda—made for much turmoils with those that were of the tribes- people. But with the establishing of the city in the plains and hills where the healing arts came, the entity then was among those of that leader's people who eventually came and aided much in the activities during that sojourn.

The entity itself aided in the aid to those that were BLINDED by the sands, the glare, and may be said to have been among the first in that particular experience and in that particular environ to make for the protecting of the eyesight by the shades, by the glass that was imported then from the Egyptian and the Indian experience.

Hence in these fields of material activity may the entity find much as a means for the expression of self in aiding others, and in bringing comfort and help—even as then; yea, as a teacher, as a director in that field may much of this WORLD'S goods come into the experience of the entity. Yet, as we find, even a greater field may be seen later; for there we find those periods when color and odor played an important part in what would be termed in present day parlance the psychological effect upon the minds of those that WOULD BE healed.

Before that we find the entity was again in the Arabian land, when the peoples journeyed into what is now called the Egyptian land. [Ra-Ta period]

The entity then was among the people that did not in the first journey to the Egyptian land, but with the establishing of the young king, with the banishment of the priest that was a relation of the entity, then Iu-Ptl-In made a journey and brought the first of the turmoils being settled with the princess and the peoples in Ibex, as an aid rather than a hindrance to the young king.

There may be particular note that those who were in that sojourn as individuals have an antipathy for the entity, and if their associations were drawn together the entity would eventually have the same character of influence upon many of those even that rebelled—or that in any way made for the troublesome periods in that experience.

Later, with the return of the priest, the entity made the drawings that would in the present be termed the commercial, architectural drawings, for much that had to do with the interior as well as exterior of the buildings.

Hence as the entity develops in body, in mind, spiritually also, if this is kept as an activity of the body in the present experience it may be made the most satisfying of the experiences—as an INTERIOR decorator, as an aide in color schemes in the various activities in home or hall, in church or in the more humble edifices in the experience. For much talent, as would be termed, that is innate may be expressed by the entity in that direction. Hence a portion of the activities of the body in its developing years should be given to such, that there may come in the experience that which may be the more helpful in the material and the mental welfare.

BETTER will the entity find it to make for self a career; not as a lone soul, rather as one with many in various associations, but not in wedded life—for such relations would bring the character of hardships that would break the purposes in the inner self.

As to what the entity may attain, and how, in the present:

Apply self first in liberty, in faith, in purity of purpose, as indicated in that which has been necessary for its activities through the earthly sojourn; bound oft by ties, bound oft by the will of others in its material activities, that the will of self must rule. Yet being made through those purposefulnesses in the ideals of an INNER urge that comes from the soul's sojourn with the Creative Forces.

Study to show thyself approved unto thy Maker, avoiding the appearances of evil, keeping the self unspotted from the world; and there will come—through the experience in this sojourn—peace, happiness, and JOY IN LIVING—as an emissary, as a light bearer for thy King—the Christ!

We are through.

Who Was Edgar Cayce?
Twentieth Century Psychic and Medical Clairvoyant

Edgar Cayce (pronounced Kay-Cee, 1877-1945) has been called the "sleeping prophet," the "father of holistic medicine," and the most-documented psychic of the 20th century. For more than 40 years of his adult life, Cayce gave psychic "readings" to thousands of seekers while in an unconscious state, diagnosing illnesses and revealing lives lived in the past and prophecies yet to come. But who, exactly, was Edgar Cayce?

Cayce was born on a farm in Hopkinsville, Kentucky, in 1877, and his psychic abilities began to appear as early as his childhood. He was able to see and talk to his late grandfather's spirit, and often played with "imaginary friends" whom he said were spirits on the other side. He also displayed an uncanny ability to memorize the pages of a book simply by sleeping on it. These gifts labeled the young Cayce as strange, but all Cayce really wanted was to help others, especially children.

Later in life, Cayce would find that he had the ability to put himself into a sleep-like state by lying down on a couch, closing his eyes, and folding his hands over his stomach. In this state of relaxation and meditation, he was able to place his mind in contact with all time and space—the universal consciousness, also known as the super-conscious mind. From there, he could respond to questions as broad as, "What are the secrets of the universe?" and "What is my purpose in life?" to as specific as, "What can I do to help my arthritis?" and "How were the pyramids of Egypt built?" His responses to these questions came to be called "readings," and their insights offer practical help and advice to individuals even today.

The majority of Edgar Cayce's readings deal with holistic health and the treatment of illness. Yet, although best known for this material, the sleeping Cayce did not seem to be limited to concerns about the physical body. In fact, in their entirety, the readings discuss an astonishing 10,000 different topics. This vast array of subject matter can be narrowed down into a smaller group of topics that, when compiled together, deal with the following five categories: (1) Health-Related Information; (2) Philosophy and Reincarnation; (3) Dreams and Dream Interpretation; (4) ESP and Psychic Phenomena; and (5) Spiritual Growth, Meditation, and Prayer.

Learn more at EdgarCayce.org.

What Is A.R.E.?

Edgar Cayce founded the non-profit Association for Research and Enlightenment, Inc. (A.R.E.®) in 1931, to explore spirituality, holistic health, intuition, dream interpretation, psychic development, reincarnation, and ancient mysteries—all subjects that frequently came up in the more than 14,000 documented psychic readings given by Cayce.

The Mission of the A.R.E. is to help people transform their lives for the better, through research, education, and application of core concepts found in the Edgar Cayce readings and kindred materials that seek to manifest the love of God and all people and promote the purposefulness of life, the oneness of God, the spiritual nature of humankind, and the connection of body, mind, and spirit.

With an international headquarters in Virginia Beach, Va., regional representatives throughout the U.S., Edgar Cayce Centers in more than thirty countries, and individual members in more than seventy countries, the A.R.E. community is a global network of individuals.

A.R.E. conferences, international tours, camps for children and adults, regional activities, and study groups allow like-minded people to gather for educational and fellowship opportunities worldwide.

A.R.E. offers membership benefits and services that include a quarterly body-mind-spirit member magazine, *Venture Inward*, a member newsletter covering the major topics of the readings, and access to the entire set of readings in an exclusive online database.

Learn more at EdgarCayce.org.Learn more at EdgarCayce.org.

EDGARCAYCE.ORG